ome Together

synago
Light in the Dark

By Karen Kluever

A Gathering

Assemble

Take in

Senior High
Student-Led
Small Groups

synago

Light in the Dark

Student-Led Senior High Small Groups

A small group ministry resource for reaching, nurturing, encouraging, and discipling senior high youth

by Karen Kluever

Scripture Credits

About the Author

Karen Kluever has a heart for teenagers. She is currently in ministry with youth at Mouzon United Methodist Church, in Charlotte, North Carolina, where she serves as director of program ministries. *Synago* comes from her experience with youth at Myers Park United Methodist, also in Charlotte, where she served as youth program coordinator for eleven years. Karen loves developing resources for youth and was the editorial assistant for *The Magazine for Christian Youth!* before moving to North Carolina. She has also written curriculum for middle school youth.

Karen has undergraduate and graduate degrees in journalism and a master's in Christian education from Pfeiffer University, in North Carolina. She is married and has three sons, ages 8, 11, and 13. (Karen says that she thinks it's great to finally have two of her own kids in youth ministry with her.)

> "I no longer call you servants. . . . Instead, I have called you friends, for everything that I learned from my Father I have made known to you. You did not choose me, but I chose you and appointed you to go and bear fruit—fruit that will last. . . . This is my command: Love each other."
>
> —Jesus
> (John 15:15-17, NIV)

What's Synago?

Synago (syn-AH-go) is the Greek word for "come together." You may recognize it as the root word of *synagogue,* a place were people come together to worship and to learn the faith. And so it is with these student-led small groups. Youth come seeking God, wanting to learn.

Synago can also be translated "to take in." One of the purposes of these student-led small groups is to reach out and invite in youth who have not been a part of a church, youth who do not have a relationship with God through Jesus Christ, youth who are seeking or perhaps struggling with faith. Friends invite friends, and the group takes them in with love.

Synago is also the root word of *synergy,* where the coming together of individual parts makes something even greater. And so it is in these small groups. In coming together to talk about their lives in light of God's good news, the group members find that something great happens.

Contents

What's Synago?

6 From the Author
7 Biblical Foundations: The Word on Small Groups

Getting Started

10 To the Ones in Charge
11 What's *Synago* All About?
12 Great Reasons for Student-Led Small Groups
13 How to Do Student-Led Small Groups
14 Typical Format
15 How to Use This Resource
16 Who's Who: Student Leader Roles and Responsibilities
17 Who's Who: Adult Roles and Responsibilities
19 Q & A

Help for Student Leaders

22 A Word of Encouragement
23 Getting Ready to Lead
24 Weekly Checklist (pre-session prep, weekly sheet)
25 Bible Study Tools You Can Use
26 Discussion Tips
28 Ways to Close in Prayer
29 It's Important! The Purpose Statement

Small Group Sessions

32 Purpose Statement
33 What's New?
    starting something new, becoming "new" in Christ
36 Child of Mine
    from childhood to adulthood, being a "child of God"
39 Stress-Less
    dealing with stress, trusting God with your needs
42 Love Story
    role of the Bible in the Christian faith
45 The Outsiders
    feeling left out, reaching out to others
48 Prayer 101
    what prayer is and how to do it
51 Getting Directions
    finding guidance for making decisions
54 What Are Friends For?
    qualities of a good friend
57 Thirst Quencher
    feeling spiritually dry or empty
60 Serve It Up
    following Jesus Christ by serving others
63 When Life Hurts
    hurting and suffering, experiencing God's comfort
66 Zip the Lip
    gossip, swearing, and obscenity
69 Loving God
    relating to God, what it means to love God
72 Loving Myself
    loving and caring for yourself
75 Loving Others
    relating to others, responding to others' needs
78 Light in the Dark
    feeling hopeless, finding hope and peace in Jesus Christ

From the Author

This resource came about, as many do, out of necessity.

While I was serving on the youth ministries staff of a large, urban church, we began to have this gnawing, restless feeling that our youth program—although "successful" in terms of variety and quality of offerings and numbers of active youth—was not successful in the way we felt it should be. We wanted to see more youth in Bible studies, mentoring relationships, and leadership roles. We wanted to see that, in addition to their participation, our youth were actually maturing in faith, growing as disciples of Jesus Christ, and living out their faith commitment in their daily lives. We wanted more than "numbers" success; we wanted "depth" success.

Convinced that small groups could provide ideal opportunities and environments for inviting, discipling, and nurturing youth in the Christian faith, we took several stabs at small group ministry over the years. We offered adult-led Bible study at church during the week; adult-led Bible study in homes during the week; and adult-led topical studies once a month at Sunday night youth group, where students were assigned to different groups to encourage building new relationships. These strategies didn't deliver — for our youth group, anyway — what we wanted them to. To paraphrase what one inventor said, We didn't make mistakes, we just learned how not to do it.

Because the small group bug was still biting, I attended a seminar on student-led cell groups. As the seminar leader described the cell group philosophy and design for student-led small groups, I knew I was close to hitting pay dirt. What sold me was the personal story-sharing of a student cell group leader. When she spoke of "ministering" to members of her cell group, in the sense of caring for them and encouraging them in the love of Christ, I imagined those same words and the passion with which they were spoken coming from my students back home.

> We wanted more than "numbers" success; we wanted "depth" success.

A team of student and adult leaders in our youth program was formed to pray about and to consider a new design for small group ministry. We checked out several models and resources. In true youth ministry fashion, we took some of this, some of that, and tossed in some of our own stuff, resulting in the design and suggestions I share with you in this resource. In developing our own format for student-led small groups, however, we "designed ourselves out" of finding curriculum that worked with our model. During our first year of student-led small groups, I modified available curriculum to fit our needs.

We felt successful with our first year's attempt. We had started the academic year with four groups and ended with eight; student leaders had stepped up to the leadership task and excelled; group members were inviting their friends (both church members and non church members); commitment to attending the weekly meetings was extremely high; our student leaders and adult counselors were enthusiastic; and we also experienced a significant increase in the number of senior high youth participating in Sunday night youth fellowship, retreats, mission trips, and so on.

In gearing up for a second year of student-led small groups, we were once again in need of a topical, Bible study resource designed for our situation. So, inspired and guided by the Spirit, with deep love and compassion for "my kids" at Myers Park Church and their friends, and out of pure necessity—the first two volumes of this curriculum for student-led senior high small groups were created. I hope that you will make it your own, using it in whatever way the Spirit leads you. Blessings!

—Karen Kluever

Biblical Foundations: The Word on Small Groups

Jesus said it. . . .

"For where two or three are gathered in my name, I am there among them."
(Matthew 18:20, NRSV)

Jesus did it. . . .

He went up the mountain and called to him those whom he wanted, and they came to him. And he appointed twelve, whom he also named apostles, to be with him, and to be sent out to proclaim the message.
(Mark 3:13-14, NRSV)

So did the first Christians. . . .

All who believed were together and had all things in common. . . . Day by day, as they spent much time together in the temple, they broke bread at home and ate their food with glad and generous hearts, praising God and having the goodwill of all the people. And day by day the Lord added to their number those who were being saved.
(Acts 2:44, 46-47, NRSV)

And there is more. . . .

"If you continue in my word, you are truly my disciples; and you will know the truth, and the truth will make you free."
(John 8:31-32, NRSV)

Therefore confess your sins to one another, and pray for one another, so that you may be healed.
(James 5:16, NRSV)

We loved you so much that we were delighted to share with you not only the gospel of God but our lives as well, because you had become so dear to us.
(1 Thessalonians 2:8, NIV)

Getting Started

To the Ones in Charge

If you are...

___ in charge of   ___ responsible for   ___ interested in

the . . .

___ supervising   ___ coordinating   ___ "selling"   ___ start up

of a senior high small group ministry in your...

___ church   ___ community   ___ organization   ___ school

and whether you are...

___ a paid youth worker   ___ a volunteer youth worker

___ not sure why someone gave you this resource and said "Good luck"

you are definitely...

___ embarking on   ___ continuing on

an exciting, high-impact adventure in youth ministry. *Synago* offers guidelines and suggestions for beginning and implementing a senior high, student-led, small group ministry, as well as providing 16 sessions for your student leaders to use in their small groups. (That's good for a semester's worth of small group meetings.)

As the person . . .

___ in charge of   ___ "volunteered for"

providing leadership for this ministry, the first section of this resource is to help you start, coordinate, and supervise *Synago* small groups.

What's Synago All About?

First and foremost, the goal of the small group is to strengthen members' spiritual relationship with God and Jesus Christ.

The sessions are led by trained student leaders, who are committed to living out, growing in, and encouraging their peers in the Christian faith. These student leaders are nurtured, supported, and supervised by one or more Christian youth workers—the counselor who is a member of their small group and possibly a small group coordinator and/or a youth ministry director.

Small group sessions are designed to help youth connect their "story" with "the Story" of the Christian faith. They discuss where their own experience and understanding of a particular life or faith issue comes together with the Scripture. Then they consider how God's love, grace, forgiveness, and call to faithfulness can have an impact upon that area of their lives.

Sessions explore topics such as anxiety, gossip, prayer, family relationships, friends, suffering, service, dating, confrontation, self-esteem, setting goals, and lots more. Generally, each session is topically based and explores one or more Bible readings, which group members analyze, interpret, and then apply to their own lives.

The second purpose of the small group is to build Christian community within a circle of friends, in which group members practice and experience what it means to be in ministry to and with one another.

The small group is friendship based. Members are not assigned to a group, but invited to the group by the group leaders or other members. Invited friends may or may not be members of the church or organization sponsoring the small group ministry, which makes this ministry an excellent way to reach beyond the walls of the church to youth who are unchurched or currently inactive.

Synago groups usually meet in the homes of group members. Since one of the goals is to reach out especially to unchurched youth, having the meeting in homes can overcome the reluctance some youth may feel about coming to something at a church building.

To encourage intimacy and trust, a policy of honesty, openmindedness, and confidentiality is communicated at each session: "What is shared in the group, stays in the group." This policy frees students to talk about very personal and sometimes painful circumstances of their lives in a loving, compassionate, and supportive environment.

Each small group has two student leaders, an adult counselor (or couple) and up to seven other student members. When there is a consistent participation of ten members, the group "multiplies" into two groups. Typically, the original co-leaders each go to one of the new groups and begin leading with a new co-leader. Additional adult leadership is then assigned to one of the new groups. Recruitment and training for both student leaders and adult counselors should happen at least two times during the year, in order to have leadership available when it comes time for a group to multiply.

For more nuts and bolts info, check out pages 13 and 19.

Great Reasons for Student-Led Small Groups

1 ## Built-in Intimacy
group members already acquainted; care about one another

2 ## Greater Commitment to the Group
because it's led by friends; friends encourage one another's attendance

3 ## More Youth Than Youth Workers
to reach other youth both in and outside the church

4 ## Leadership Development
especially of the student leaders

5 ## Biblical Roots
the disciples and early Christian church

6 ## Youth Drawn to Christ Through Their Circle of Friends
by their love, care, encouragement, and support

How to Do Student-Led Small Groups

- Meet once a week.
- Meet in homes of group members (may stay at one location for 2–4 weeks).
- Meet for 1½ hours. The day and time is to be determined by co-leaders (who may have the input of group members).
- Have two student co-leaders.
- Have at least one adult counselor. (There may be two counselors.)
- Have a spiritual mix (see below).
- Maintain the group at a maximum of ten regular members. If the group grows beyond ten members, multiply into two groups.
- Grow by inviting friends.
- Use topical sessions with faith applications
- Maintain the group as a safe, confidential place to gather as a faith community.

Spiritual Mix

What is a spiritual mix? Each group should strive for a mix of members at different levels of faith maturity. By intentionally keeping the group open to all persons, the members help one another. Everyone brings something to the group; everyone gains something from the group.

Non-Christians and New Converts

Non-Christians and new converts need care and encouragement from the small group. With their searching questions and interest in learning about Christianity, these youth challenge the more mature Christians to reflect on and articulate their faith and spiritual experiences in a way that makes sense to others who do not share the same experiences or faith language.

Struggling Christians

Struggling Christians are those who have made a commitment to the Christian faith but who are dealing with one or more serious problems with family, school, friends, faith, and so forth. They also need care and encouragement from group members during a difficult time in their lives. The small group will be a safe place to talk about their problems and to receive God's care, support, and healing through the loving expressions of other group members.

Strong Christians

These students should be encouraged to continue growing in their faith and living it out in all the areas of their lives. They should be expected to accept specific leadership roles in the small group or in other ministries of the church. As they are faced with the needs and questions of group members with little or no Christian background, or who are struggling with issues in their lives, the stronger Christians will have opportunities to share God's love with friends and encourage them with their own faith stories.

Typical Format

15 minutes ----> Socializing
Don't forget the snacks.

5 minutes ----> Opening
Welcome new members.
Make announcements (such as upcoming youth group
and church activities).
Read Purpose Statement.
Pray together.

8 minutes ----> Warm-Up
Start the group thinking.

15 minutes ----> Topic Talk
Introduce and get into the topic.

15 minutes ----> Word Search
Read and examine the biblical text.

15 minutes ----> R & R—Reflect and Respond
Discuss personal applications.

2 minutes ----> Wrap-Up
Review main points.

10 minutes ----> Celebrations and Concerns
Take time to share.

5 minutes ----> Closing
Pray together.

1½ hours total

Synago: Light in the Dark

How to Use This Resource

This book is one in a series of resources that will help you successfully begin and continue an effective small group ministry for senior high youth. Each volume gives sixteen sessions (a semester's worth) that are topical Bible studies. Each volume has the same start-up information and helps for student leaders, so you may begin with any volume. Both of the student leaders and the adults who are working with the group(s) will want to have a copy.

Synago: Light in the Dark (student leader)
ISBN: 0687049334
Synago: Calm in the Storm (student leader)
ISBN: 0687049237

For future volumes, see ileadyouth.com.

The **training video** is also for both the adults working with the group(s) and the student leaders. It is best to view it together so that both the leaders and adults understand their roles and responsibilities and can fully support one another.

Synago Training Video
ISBN:0687050235

The **small group notebook** is the hands-on piece for everyone. Provide copies to student leaders, adult counselors, and the other youth members of each small group. The notebook contains the Scripture readings for each session, personal reflection and response activities for the week, and space for note taking and recording prayer requests.

Synago: Light in the Dark (student notebook)
ISBN: 0687049733
Synago: Calm in the Storm (student notebook)
ISBN: 0687049539

For future volumes, see ileadyouth.com.

The **introductory video** is a great way to generate excitement and support for starting your student-led small group ministry. Use it to recruit student leaders and adult counselors and to publicize your small group ministry to parents, pastors, and others whose support you'll need.

Synago Introductory Video
ISBN:068704913X

Tips

Check for Fit
Carefully and prayerfully read through this resource to determine if it offers you a model and study material that fits your vision for senior high small group ministry. If it does, use it with the Spirit's guidance to develop your own small group ministry for senior high youth.

Recruit and Train, Practice and Publicize
Use the info in the "Getting Started" and "Help for Student Leaders" sections (pages 9–19 and 22–29) to recruit and train student leaders and adult counselors. You have permission to photocopy certain pages, as noted, in these sections for overhead transparencies and handouts you may want to use for orientation or training. A very effective way to do training is for potential leaders and counselors to experience being a small group. Use one or more of the small group sessions for practice and/or to show what the small group meetings will be like.

Who's Who: Student Leader Roles and Responsibilities

There are two student leaders for each small group; they share the leadership responsibilities, taking turns preparing for and leading the weekly meeting.

Length of Service: One academic year, or through the end of current school year

Qualities: Committed Christian who actively seeks to grow in and live out the Christian faith*; is willing to be discipled as a Christian and trained as a group leader; attends church regularly; relates well with others; is responsible; is a "team player"; is a good communicator; desires to see friends and peers learn about, experience, and grow in the Christian faith; is willing and able to make the time commitment needed for this role.

Responsibilities:

- Attends weekly small group meeting and small group leadership meetings, as scheduled.
- Prepares for the meeting. One leader is responsible for facilitating (session material provided in this resource). The other leader is responsible for the other meeting preparations and follow-up (listed below). These roles alternate each week or the leaders may take turns leading different sections within each session.
- Invites non-Christian friends, Christian friends not active in a church (or who attend a church with few youth opportunities), and youth in need of a loving and caring group of friends; encourages other group members to do this too.
- Reminds group members and potential visitors of meeting time and location.
- Helps arrange transportation for those who need it.
- If facilitating, prepares for the session using the material provided in this resource and the student notebook. (The leader who isn't facilitating still reads through the session material to be prepared to participate in the discussion and help the facilitator if needed.)
- Records attendance and collects visitor contact information; if there is a small group coordinator, forwards the information to him or her within two days.

- Follows up with visitors within two days (by calling, e-mailing, or talking to them at school).
- Follows up with those absent.
- Keeps small group coordinator updated about condition and progress of group.
- Prays regularly for the group and group members.
- Reaches out to group members in special need of the support and care of a Christian friend.
- Encourages group members to have a positive attitude towards the group growing and "multiplying."
- Keeps an eye out for potential new student leaders from within the group.
- Works with co-leader, counselor, and small group coordinator to plan how the group can "multiply" when it reaches ten regular members and works to make the transition a smooth one.

*Note to Student Leaders:

Your desire as a Christian, especially as a small group leader, is to live in such a way that others will see the qualities and "fruit" of a Christian life. Try as hard as you can to not do or say anything that would cause others to question your commitment or that might encourage them to do or say things that are unChristian. We're talking about anything that could harm your (or your peers') relationship with God or with others, or that could harm yourself or others—like drinking, smoking, abusing drugs, lying, fighting, gossiping, being sexually promiscuous, cheating, cursing, and so on. A leader cannot be a "roller coaster" Christian — one who professes a commitment to Christ and acts very devout at times, then parties like crazy on the weekend. Your group members, and peers who may be observing you from a distance, are checking out whether your words match your actions. They want to see if your faith is real. If you're a fake, they will know it, and you'll lose credibility and integrity as a small group leader and as a follower of Christ. However, nobody is perfect, and you will mess up. But don't give up! As Christians, we know that "if we confess our sins, [God] will forgive our sin, because we can trust God to do what is right. God will cleanse us from all the wrongs we have done" (1 John 1:9, NIV). Seek the support of your small group, your counselor, small group coordinator, and youth director to help you grow in Christian maturity and to faithfully live out your commitment.

Person in Charge: Vision Keeper

- Shapes and communicates the vision for the small group ministry, its purpose, and how it fits into the total youth ministry program.
- Takes overall responsibility for the small group ministry, in terms of leader accountability, resources, training, spiritual nurture. In other words, "the buck stops here."
- Has a good idea of what is going on in general, but not closely involved in the details of individual groups.
- Guides and helps student leaders, counselors, and coordinators as needed.
- Plans and leads small group leadership meetings.
- Communicates information about small groups to potential group members and provides a way for senior high youth at the church to indicate their interest in being in a group. (Can delegate this task to a small group coordinator.)

> In some situations the vision keeper, coordinator, and counselor roles can all be handled by one person. But plan to grow. Share the vision. Bring other adults on board so that as the numbers of groups grow, adults will be ready to support the ministry.

Small Group Coordinator

Length of Service: One academic year, or through the end of current school year

Qualities: Committed Christian who actively seeks to grow in and live out the Christian faith, attends church regularly, relates well with others, is a good communicator, has administrative and organizational abilities, is interested in discipling students, and is willing to commit the time and energy needed for this role.

Responsibilities:

- Supervises, nurtures, and encourages the leadership of one to four small groups.
- Serves as liaison between his or her small groups and the youth director or whoever is the vision keeper.
- Helps plan and lead orientation and training events.
- Helps with small group leadership meetings.
- Guides and helps student leaders and counselors with issues or problems in their groups or their personal lives.
- Keeps up with the attendance and membership numbers of his or her small groups, tracking to anticipate when it is time to "birth" new groups.
- Helps groups that are "multiplying" by working with leaders and counselors in choosing and training new leadership, deciding who's in the new groups and who their leaders and counselors will be, and doing whatever is needed for a smooth transition.
- Keeps current roster of members of his or her groups, along with address, phone number, e-mail, and other info; forwards this to the youth director for updating youth database.
- Provides leaders with visitor cards or other tool for collecting and reporting visitor info (name, address, phone, e-mail, school, grade, parents, church affiliation, who invited them, and so on).
- Substitutes for counselors at group meetings when needed.
- Regularly contacts his or her student leaders and counselors to keep up with what's happening in their groups.

Adult Counselor

The adult counselor is the key behind-the-scenes person who supports the student leaders by encouraging and advising them and being a caring adult friend.

The counselor doesn't prepare or lead the session. Rather, he or she participates on the same level as the student small group members.

Although the counselor can speak from an adult perspective—and the students may, at times, specifically ask for that perspective—the counselor should not monopolize the discussion, act as a facilitator, or "take the stage" as the one with the "right" answers.

Length of Service: One academic year, or through the end of current school year

Qualities: Committed Christian, actively seeks to grow in and live out the Christian faith, attends church regularly, relates well to others, is a good communicator, is interested in discipling students, is willing and able to make the time commitment needed for this role.

Responsibilities:
- Supports and encourages student leaders as an adult Christian friend; affirms their leadership and offers helpful input; checks regularly to see how they're doing and to encourage their spiritual growth; holds them accountable for actively seeking spiritual growth and fulfilling their leader responsibilities.
- Attends weekly group meetings and leadership meetings, as scheduled.

- Finds another adult to substitute for him or her at a small group meeting if he or she has to miss. (The substitute could be the small group coordinator, another counselor, or the youth director.)
- Reviews the session material to prepare for the discussion and to help and encourage the student leaders, as needed.
- Follows up with student leaders to make sure that the session is prepared, home is lined up, and the meeting time and place are communicated to group members.
- Encourages leaders to specifically invite non-Christian friends and Christian friends not active in a church (or who attend a church with few youth opportunities), and youth in need of a loving and caring group of friends.
- Reaches out to group members in special need of the support and care of an adult Christian friend.
- Encourages leaders to have a positive attitude toward the group growing and "multiplying."
- Keeps an eye out for potential new student leaders from within the group.
- Collects visitor information (address, phone, e-mail, school, grade, parent(s), church affiliation, group member who invited them, and so forth).
- Writes or calls the parent(s) of visitors to introduce self and give general information about the small group, sponsoring church, and answer any questions.
- Updates small group coordinator about condition and progress of group, student leaders, and any group members in special need.

Most groups do very well with only one counselor. However, groups also benefit from having a male and a female adult with them. When recruiting, consider inviting a couple to fill this role.

Synago: Light in the Dark

Q Is *Synago* just for large churches?

A Any church, large or small, can launch a small group ministry. Since this design is friendship based, a church is not limited by its youth membership base. The only limitation is the number of Christian youth committed to growing in their faith and willing to take on the leading and nurturing of a group of their friends and by the number of adults willing to serve as counselors. Where two or three are gathered together, there can be a small group.

Q Why don't we just do *Synago* on Sunday morning at the church?

A For many youth, small groups help break barriers to connecting to the church—barriers caused by unfamiliarity, a negative church experience in the past, or negative stereotypes of church or of Christians. Once a youth has reached high school, it's awkward for him or her to suddenly start showing up at youth group or Sunday school. With a small group, youth grow close to the other members. Then going to a larger fellowship of youth—such as Sunday school, youth group, retreats, and worship—isn't so intimidating because they know their friends from the small group are there. Doing announcements in the small group and adding the members to e-mail and mailing lists are ways to continue to invite them to participate in other youth activities and in the congregation.

Q Is *Synago* for all of the high school students in our church?

A Starting a small group ministry doesn't mean stopping Sunday school, youth group, or whatever else your church is offering older youth. This new ministry simply adds a different dimension to what is already in place. *Synago* may not be for all of those who are already active; but some youth will be ready for the greater challenge of leadership, and others will desire the intimacy of a small group. *Synago* may also reach some older youth who have not had their needs met in existing programs and consequently have stopped coming. These youth may find this format to be more what they need. In addition, *Synago* may reach new youth. The in-home, small group setting provides a way for youth—especially those who would never darken the door of a church—to connect and grow spiritually. This friendship-based model offers a unique avenue for evangelism and for greater discipleship.

Q Do we have to do the sessions in order?

A There is a flow to the sessions in each book. The early ones intentionally provide opportunities for the members to get to know one another better. The last one gives the group some closure. However, each session stands on its own. New youth will be coming into the group at different points in the life of the group. So, what is more important than the order of the sessions is the "order" of the group—the atmosphere of caring and of learning together. Do the sessions in the order that makes sense to you as the leaders.

Q Our group has gotten so close. Do we really have to split up?

A The first time your group grows to the point that it needs to "multiply" will be challenging. But if a group grows too large, many of the benefits of being a small and close-knit are lost. One reason for repeating the Purpose Statement at each meeting is to prepare the group. The leaders' having a positive attitude and also involving the group in deciding how to divide are crucial to making the multiplying go smoothly. When your group is ready to multiply, have a "birth day" celebration.

A Word of Encouragement: You Can Do It!

Feeling a little nervous about leading a small group? A bit overwhelmed? Wondering if you'll be able to keep discussions alive? What if friends you invite don't come? What if you get asked questions about God or Jesus or the Bible and you don't know the answers? Don't worry. You can do this! Here's why:

- **You've been chosen.** Someone has seen in you a love for God, devotion to Jesus Christ, a desire to grow spiritually, and compassion for your teenage peers. Someone already believes in your ability to be a small group leader. That's why you were asked to be a student leader. Jesus Christ has also chosen you, as one of his disciples. He will equip you and empower you as you seek to live as his follower and to use your gifts and abilities in his service.

- **You are not alone.** You will have the support and encouragement of others—your co-leader, counselor, small group coordinator, and youth director or pastor. Call on them when you need advice, help, or just a friend to talk to. You are part of a ministry team.

- **You don't have to be an expert.** A student leader should have a love for God's Word, not a mastery of it. You should have a desire to learn more about the Bible and how to apply its truth and teachings to your life. You'll learn a lot about the Bible as you prepare to lead your group, and you'll have opportunities to share information that may be helpful to others during your study of biblical passages. If you're asked a question you can't answer, just promise to check into it and get back with what you find out. Perhaps someone else in the group has an answer. If not, do a little research (Bible commentaries, pastor or other Christian adult) and report what you find out.

- **You can learn.** Your training as a student leader and the tips provided in this resource will help prepare you to lead meaningful and productive discussions. You'll also get practical advice at leadership meetings, as you and other small group leaders talk about what works in your groups and exchange ideas. You'll also become better at facilitating as you gain experience and get to know and understand your group's dynamics.

- **You can expect great meetings and not-so-great meetings.** Sometimes even the best preparation and most skillful discussion-leading won't result in a great meeting. Sometimes your group may just be in a funk and not be talkative—or the opposite—everyone has the sillies and can't get serious. You may have a meeting where, for whatever reasons, you have a much lower turn-out than normal. Sometimes there may be distractions over which you have no control. "Dud" meetings aren't a sign of personal failure on your part. They just happen. Keep a positive attitude, and don't be discouraged. Consider what God can teach you through the experience.

- **You have something special to offer—yourself.** No one is in a better position to reach out to and connect with your friends and peers than YOU. They know you; they like you; they trust you. You'll be an awesome student leader, if you're willing to just be yourself—a Christian teen who doesn't have all the answers, but who does have a faith story to share; who isn't perfect, but who believes in forgiveness and hanging in there; and who is kind and compassionate to others.

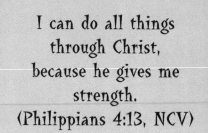

I can do all things through Christ, because he gives me strength.
(Philippians 4:13, NCV)

Session Prep

Start preparing days (not hours) before your small group meeting. Putting time into your preparation

1. reflects your commitment to the group;
2. helps you to be mentally and spiritually ready to lead and participate in the session;
3. makes it less likely that you will forget something (like supplies, or letting group members know of a location change); and
4. results in a more smoothly-run session, as you have time to get comfortable with the session material and are better able to encourage and contribute to the discussion.

By getting an early start on your preparation, you'll also have time to consult with your counselor, in case you have any questions or concerns. Although you can do a lot of the prep work by yourself, you and your co-leader should spend some time preparing together and sharing the responsibilities, so you know who's doing what and can make sure that nothing on the checklist gets overlooked.

Personal Prep

Try to spend at least ten to fifteen minutes a day with God in a personal devotional time. Your *Synago* Notebook has some questions and activities for reflection and response that you can use for devotionals. The group members will be doing them the week after your meeting, but you will find that doing them the week before is helpful to you as you lead.

You may also use a devotional book or read a Bible passage that you can pray about, reflect on, and/or write about in a journal. Spend time each day praying to God, expressing thanks and praise, confessing your sins, and asking for forgiveness and guidance. Pray for your own needs and for those of your small group members. Pray for your session time together.

Last Minute Details!

- Get your supplies—pens, *Synago* Notebooks, extra Bibles, and so on.
- Arrive fifteen minutes early. You need to have time to greet the host family, set up the meeting area, get focused, and welcome group members as they arrive.
- Set up the meeting area so everyone can sit in a circle. Control for distractions, such as TV and stereo, pets or children, and phones.

R&R in the Synago Notebook

Every participant should have a notebook. It contains the Scripture, a place for notes, room to write in prayer requests—and some simple R&R (Reflect and Respond) for during the week. As part of your closing time each session, remind the participants of the R&R section and invite them to continue their spiritual growth between meetings.

If for some reason your planned material is not taking as much time as is available, turn to the R&R directions in the notebook for more ideas for the session. Doing R&R together is a good way to encourage one another to develop some practices that will continue to help you grow in your faith and devotion to God.

Weekly Checklist

These things need to happen before each meeting. Coordinate with your co-leader.

___ Maintain **attendance** record of last meeting.

___ Give a **thank-you call** to the host parents of your last meeting location.

___ Follow up, within two days, with **visitors** to your last meeting (by phone, e-mail, card, talking at school). This means telling them you're glad they came and appreciated their participation; giving them additional info about the group or answering any questions they may have; inviting them to come again; asking if they have anything going on in their lives that you can be praying about for them.

___ Find out if anyone needs a ride; help make **arrangements**, if necessary.

___ If you have a new, regular group member, get a **Synago Notebook** for him or her.

___ Bring some **Bibles**. The Scriptures are all printed in the *Synago* Notebook, so everyone can read them easily with no one being embarrassed about not knowing where to find them in the Bible. But as participants grow more confident, encourage them to bring and use their Bibles or the ones on hand. Besides, it's fun and often very helpful to see how the different versions translate a passage.

___ Follow up with group **members who missed** the last meeting.

___ Confirm the **next meeting place** (home) and refreshments.

___ Contact (call, e-mail, tell at school) **group members** to make sure that they know where you're meeting. Remind them to bring their *Synago* Notebooks (or Bibles).

___ As often as you can, invite **friends and acquaintances** who are non-Christians, not involved with a church, or Christian youth having personal struggles. You set an important example for others in your group. If you don't invite anyone, why should they? Encourage your group members to be invitational by your words and your actions.

___ Check in with your **counselor**. Evaluate your last meeting. Go over anything you need to for the next one.

___ Think about and get any **supplies** you may need.

___ Work through the **session material** for the next meeting. Highlight key points; do some research on unfamiliar words, phrases, verses. The *Synago* Notebook includes the text for the Bible passages and has margin notes with helpful information. You can also look the texts up in a Bible dictionary or commentary. Talk to your counselor, small group coordinator, or youth director, or pastor about anything you don't understand or want more information on. It's great to ask questions! That's how you learn!

Synago: Light in the Dark

Bible Study Tools You Can Use

The Bible

Although the Scripture for each session is printed in the *Synago* Notebook, you need a Bible to help prepare for the "Word Search" (Bible study) part of your small group meeting. You also need a Bible for your personal reading, study, and devotional times. Some Bibles are easier to read and understand than others. In fact, some Bibles are designed especially for youth. Here are some things to keep in mind when getting a Bible:

Translation—In a Bible translation, the original Hebrew or Greek text has been translated into another language, like English. Some translations you may have heard of are the New Revised Standard Version (NRSV), New International Version (NIV), New King James Version (NJKV), and the Contemporary English Version (CEV). But how can you have several translations of the same text, you ask? Say you've been given a story in your Spanish class that you have to translate from Spanish into English. When all the papers are turned in, the translations may differ slightly according to the words and phrases different students choose to use. Sometimes reading the same passage in different versions can help make the meaning clearer.

Paraphrase—A paraphrase of the Bible tends to be written in contemporary language, making it readable, colorful, and easy to understand. Unlike a translation, it isn't a direct translation of the original. Instead, a paraphrase restates what the text means. Paraphrases use contemporary words, phrases, metaphors, and images that have meaning within the times and culture of the reader, not the times and culture of the writings. *The Message* and *The Living Bible* are examples of paraphrases.

Study Bible—A study Bible is available in different translations. It has notes on specific Bible verses, definitions of unfamiliar words, and information on Bible people, Bible lands, and Bible times to help you understand the meaning and interpretation of biblical texts. Some study Bibles also have devotional material and questions for reflection and personal application.

Dictionaries and Commentaries

These books are like having a knowledgeable person right there to help you answer questions or give another viewpoint.

Bible Dictionary—This gives definitions for tons of words found in the Bible. This is especially helpful if you don't have a study Bible.

Commentary—This resource gives you someone's scholarly understanding and interpretation of Scripture. It includes explanations and cultural information, as well as information about who probably wrote the text, why, and for whom it was written. Commentaries can help you understand why certain stories were told, events recorded, or teachings given and what significance they had for the original audience (who heard them about two thousand years ago in the Middle East). If you don't have a Bible commentary at home, try your church or a library.

Voice, Audience, Context

In your role as a student leader, you're expected to spend time learning what you can about the Scripture passage for the session, so you can help others in your group gain a better understanding or help them consider a different meaning or interpretation. Your preparation should include determining the voice, audience, and context of the text your group is studying.

Voice—Who was the writer? Or who is "speaking" in the passage?

Audience—Who was listening? Who were the ones hearing the words originally? For whom was the text originally written?

Context—What comes before and after the text? How does this add to the meaning and significance of the text? Also what was the society of that time like? What was the context in which the people lived and would have understood what was being said? What do you know about the times and the people back then?

Answering these questions also helps prevent prooftexting. Prooftexting is taking Scripture out of context and applying it or using it in a way that wasn't originally intended or that is inconsistent with the overall message of the Bible—the story of God's love for us.

Discussion Tips

One reason your group members will keep coming to your small group is the opportunity to talk with friends about a topic of personal interest and share things of a personal nature in a safe and confidential environment. You, as a student leader, are key to creating that environment by reminding everyone of the confidential nature of the discussions and by encouraging honesty and openmindedness. Here are some specific suggestions to get them talking and to keep them coming back to your small group meetings!

DO know that your role is to facilitate, or help, not to be an expert. In other words, you don't have to have all the answers! Your job is to encourage sharing and reflection among group members, presenting helpful information that will add to their understanding and ability to participate. Although you have prepared for the session and done some research on the biblical text, it's very likely that someone will ask a question to which you don't know the answer. When that happens, toss it back to the group and see if anyone else has a response. You can also offer to look into it, or have another member check it out, and come back the next week with some more information. This gives you time to check with your youth director, pastor, or another source who may be able to help you. You may also be dealing with a question that you just need to say is "unanswerable."

DON'T be afraid of silence. To give thoughtful, honest answers, group members will often need time to reflect and think of what they want to say. If you feel the silence is getting too long, try rephrasing the question. If the answer involves some personal sharing, you may need to go first (which is why you need to have thought through your own answers ahead of time!). Your example of being open, honest, vulnerable, and trusting will encourage others to be the same.

DO try to avoid the student/teacher syndrome. Since you've already prepared your own responses to the questions, you may be tempted to want to give your answers first, especially if you encounter some silence. Resist that temptation. Instead, be OK with a little silence, encourage your friends to take some time to reflect, or ask "What do you guys think?" Sometimes, group members may try to give you the answer they think you're looking for—an answer that "sounds" right. For example, if you're asking a question about the biblical text, they may look at

you as they answer to see if they got it "right." Although there will be some key points that certain questions will attempt to bring out in the discussion, try to work in these points yourself only if others haven't.

DON'T be judgmental or critical about others' comments. (In other words, don't laugh at a comment that wasn't meant to be funny; don't express horror, shock, or disgust with what someone says; don't say, "That is so stupid; where did you get that idea?" or "I can't believe you really believe that!") Set an example of openmindedness and encourage it in the discussion. If someone says something insensitive, insulting, or really surprising, ask if anyone else has a response (without being insensitive or insulting themselves). Sometimes you may need to help group members decide to "agree to disagree" about something. You may also want to ask follow-up questions to help individuals consider why they have a particular belief or opinion and where it came from.

DO "peel the onion." Sometimes people have difficulty expressing themselves or communicating what they mean. If you don't understand a group member's comment, you may need to ask follow-up questions to help him or her explain an answer. You can "peel the onion," or get more info from someone, by asking questions like, "Can you give me an example of what you're talking about?"; "I think I know what you're getting at, but I'm not sure. Can you think of another way to say that to help me understand?" "That's a very interesting way of looking at it. What helped you come up with that interpretation?"

DO control gossips, side conversations, and discussion hogs. These are major discussion killers. This may be hard for you to do as a student leader, because the people in your group are your peers. It's uncomfortable for many teens to act like an authority figure with their friends. But as a group leader, it is your responsibility, not the adult counselor's, to keep the discussion focused, moving along, and productive. It is also your job to promote a safe and confidential environment, so that group members will want to talk. You, your co-leader, and counselor should come up with strategies for dealing with these situations, with specific ideas for what to say or do. You may even want to address this in your group and get group members' input on how do deal with these situations when they happen. If you have an ongoing problem with one or more individuals and none of your strategies have worked, then speak with them privately and in a nonjudgmental manner, relating your concerns and suggesting how they can help.

DO know when to ask and when to wait. Sometimes it's OK to ask specific group members to respond and sometimes you need to let a question "hang out there" for voluntary answers. There are questions in each session that everyone should feel comfortable answering. These questions have an asterisk (*) by them. Encourage each person to answer these. ("OK, guys, this is a question for each of us to answer"; "Joe, we haven't heard from you. How would you answer this question?") But, of course, you can't force someone to answer, and you never want to make anyone feel uncomfortable for choosing not to participate.

Most of the session questions, however, are designed for group members to answer voluntarily. (Introduce those questions with, "This next one's for the whole group." Or follow-up the question with, "Does anyone else have an answer for this one?")

Also, make sure that you only ask volunteers to read the biblical text in the session. Some people just aren't comfortable reading out loud, and you might not know who is or who isn't. Same goes for prayer. You may want to ask for volunteers to open and close your closing prayer time. During this time, prayer is offered aloud voluntarily. There are some options for the closing prayer, however, that do require each person to participate. Typically, though, this only involves saying a one-word prayer or praying for someone by just repeating a phrase or mentioning a name (like, "Pray for the person on your right by saying, 'Thank you, God, for _____.' ").

DO encourage and set an example of being a good listener. Don't have a side conversation with your co-leader while someone in your group is talking. Show compassion and understanding; be honest and open. Also be openminded and accepting of opinions and beliefs that differ from or are even in conflict with yours.

DO watch the clock; keep the discussion focused. This will be hard. Group discussions can easily jump from one topic to another, taking up lots of time and getting way off track. Plus, some people are just long-winded. Keep the discussion moving and focused. As you prepare for the session, have a good idea of how much time to spend on each part. (You may even want to write down the times in the margin, such as "7:15–7:20" beside "Warm-Up.") Decide, in advance, which questions you may need to "ax," if you run short on time. The goal is to make sure you don't spend so much time on the Warm-Up and Topic Talk sections (which group members can really get into), that you run out of time for the biblical study, reflection, sharing of personal concerns, and prayer time. These are the sections that provide the most opportunities for your group to talk about things that are private, to share their faith stories and experiences, to be reflective, and to show love and concern to each other as a faith community.

DO consistently stress the importance of confidentiality. If anyone tells something said in small group to a friend, parent, teacher, coach who isn't in the group, then confidentiality is violated. This can kill a small group. If this happens, depending on the nature of what was told, you and your co-leader and counselor must decide how to respond. The only exception to the rule of confidentiality is when a group member says something that indicates that he or she or others may be in danger. (This includes references to suicide, abuse, harming self or others, or running away.) If this happens, the counselor should give this information to the youth director or pastor, who will determine the appropriate action.

Discussion Tips

Ways to Close in Prayer

Choose in Advance

Most of the sessions give you the choice of how to close in prayer. In making that choice, you'll need to consider the number of persons in your group (a lot or a few, since this affects your time), make up of group (comfort level with praying aloud), session topic, and amount of remaining time. Because you can't predict what can happen in a session that will affect the timing and mood, you'll need to be flexible and ready to adapt or change your prayer closing.

Write 'Em Down

Before your closing prayer, your group will spend time sharing personal celebrations (great things that have recently happened, answered prayer) and prayer concerns (things for which they'd like the group to pray). During this time, you and the other members should write down the specific prayer requests in your *Synago* Notebooks so you can pray for these concerns during the week.

Encourage Others

Your closing prayer time is a great opportunity to encourage your group in their own prayer life. Some members may feel they aren't "good" at praying. (Maybe you feel that way!) This is a good time to remind everyone that prayer is simply talking to God. You don't need to use certain words or sound eloquent. God already knows our requests before we ask. It's not the words that make great prayers; it's the honesty and sincerity with which they're offered. Encourage the group just to pray as if they were talking to a close friend.

Options for Closing Prayers

Solo Prayer

A leader or member prays. This style is best to use when you're running short on time—but don't overuse it!

Pulse Prayer

Everyone holds hands. Starting with a leader and moving to the person on the right, each person prays either aloud *or* silently. When finished, each person squeezes the hand of the person to his or her right, indicating it's that person's turn to pray. The last person closes with "Amen."

Shared Prayer

After group members have given prayer concerns, the leader asks for a volunteer to choose and pray for a specific concern. (For example, Zach volunteers to pray for Meredith's sick grandmother.) The last person to pray should cover any concern not already prayed for by other group members.

Popcorn Prayer

Ask for two volunteers to open and close the prayer. (If you know some people in your group who are comfortable praying aloud, you may want to ask them. Just don't have the same people opening and closing all the time.) After someone has opened in prayer, anyone who wants to pray aloud does so at will. Persons can "go" more than once. When a long silence indicates the group's readiness to close, the "closer" wraps up.

Prayer Box

Have a small box or basket or cap out during the meeting, along with some pens and scratch paper. Encourage persons to write down a prayer request or celebration as one comes to mind and to put it in the prayer box. They can include their name with their request or remain anonymous. You could also choose to have members do this during the "Celebrations and Concerns" time. For the closing prayer, each person picks one of the prayer requests and prays aloud for it. Remind the group that praying for the request can be simply reading it aloud from the paper, perhaps with a follow-up chorus of "Hear our prayer, O Lord."

It's Important! The Purpose Statement

Reading the Purpose Statement at the beginning of each session is extremely important. If group members have heard it enough to know it by heart, that's even better! Here's why you should not skip opening with reading the Purpose Statement:

- It focuses everyone on why they are a small group and what is supposed to happen in the session. It communicates expectations for personal behavior (honest, openminded, encouraging), goals for personal spiritual growth, and goals for the group to grow together as a body of Christ.

- It keeps the group Christ-centered. Although the meeting provides a place to openly discuss differing opinions, interpretations, and beliefs, the story of the Christian faith and the teachings of Christ take center stage. The discussion is an opportunity to reflect on the Christian faith as it relates to their personal opinions, experiences, and issues.

- It spells out expectations that the group live as a faith community, following biblical teachings for believers. You can call these the "One Another Principles": love one another, be kind to one another, pray for one another, forgive one another, encourage one another.

- It informs visitors that you are a Christian group. Even though your membership is open to and encourages participation of youth who are not Christian or who are not active in church, you want visitors to know up front that they will be exploring life issues in relation to the Christian faith. Your small group members may invite friends by saying that you get together and talk about stuff, leaving out the Jesus Christ part. But by hearing the Purpose Statement, visitors are clearly informed.

- It reaffirms the confidential nature of the group. Group members are reminded of their personal responsibility to keep confidentiality. Stressing this communicates that the small group is a safe place for sharing.

- It communicates the goal to grow in numbers, in order to "multiply" into new groups. Because your members may become very close, they may lose sight of the goal to bring others into the group and may become resistant to growth and change. This mindset leads to a group that is exclusive, rather than invitational. They become more focused on staying together, rather than on sharing with others what they've found in their small group experience. The group is designed to grow. Reading the Purpose Statement reminds your group of this goal, so that when time comes to multiply into two new groups, it's not a shock.

Purpose Statement

The Purposes of Our Small Group Are to

- grow closer in our relationships with God and Jesus Christ;

- grow closer in our relationships with one another;

- learn more about the Christian faith and God's Word;

- encourage honesty and sharing in an atmosphere of trust, confidentiality, and open-mindedness;

- support one another and care for one another in Christian love;

- grow in number by inviting others;

- "multiply" into two groups when we reach 10 regular members to encourage intimacy and continued growth.

Small Group Sessions

The purposes of our small group are to

Grow closer in our relationships with God
and Jesus Christ;

Grow closer in our relationships
with one another;

Learn more about the Christian faith
and God's Word;

Encourage honesty and sharing
in an atmosphere of trust, confidentiality,
and open-mindedness

Support one another and care
for one another in Christian love;

Grow in number by inviting others;

"Multiply" into two groups when we reach 10
regular members to encourage intimacy and
continued growth.

Life Issue

Starting something new—how you feel about it and deal with it

Faith Connection

The concept of "newness" is both positive and biblical. Whether we are becoming a new person, following a "new" commandment, or making a new start, God's Spirit inspires us and enables us to be transformed into "new and improved" people.

Main Ideas

What's new? You may be constantly finding yourself either starting something new or having to deal with something new—new school year, new school), new classes, new family situation, new job, new friends, new styles, new small group. You may look forward to new situations and experiences, or you may want to avoid them.

Newness isn't limited to only what's happening around you. A lot of change is going on inside you, too, as you grow at a phenomenal rate physically, emotionally, mentally, and spiritually during your teen years. You can choose to look positively at new situations, to see them as opportunities for personal growth, if you consider that God created us and wants to continually transform us into better human beings.

God desires that we become "new and improved" in our lives and in our faith. And the great news is that God doesn't leave it completely up to us to do the transforming. Rather, the Spirit of God is at work in our lives, shaping us into the people God envisions us and calls us to be—doing God's work, showing God's love, experiencing God's blessings, and giving praise to our God.

Read, Research, Reflect
Ezekiel 36:26; Psalm 40:1-3; John 13:34; Colossians 3:9-10

Read the Scripture passages and the additional info in your *Synago* Notebook. Make notes on the following:

- Who is speaking or telling the story in each passage? Who is the intended audience? What is the context? (What do you think the situation is? What's happening before and after this passage?)
- Pray about and reflect on the reading. What does it say to you?

Memorize

*He put a new song in my mouth, a song of praise to our God.
(Psalm 40:3)*

Prepare

- Note your own answers to the questions.
- Decide how you'll close in prayer. (See "Ways to Close in Prayer," page 28.)
- Get supplies.

Session Plan

Supplies: *Synago* Notebook for each person, pencils or pens, Bibles or copies of the Bible readings and note cards for those who don't have a *Synago* Notebook

Opening   5 minutes

Welcome/Announcements/Purpose Statement/Prayer

Warm-Up   5 minutes

Hand out *Synago* Notebooks (or note cards) and pencils or pens. Ask the group members to draw a tattoo design that says something about who they are, such as something they're good at or enjoy doing, their personality, something they value, and so forth. Take a minute to let the members draw their designs, then to let them briefly show the designs to the group and tell about them.

Topic Talk   15 minutes

* *Questions with an * should be answered by everyone.*

1. Tell about something new that has recently happened or is happening in your life. What kind of impact is it having?*

2. How do you typically react in new situations or experiences? (cautious, flexible, reserved, assertive, and so forth) Give an example. Why do you typically act this way?

3. If you could really become a "new" person, what is one change you'd like to see in the "new" you that isn't a physical change?*

Word Search   20 minutes
Ezekiel 36:26; Psalm 40:1-3; John 13:34; Colossians 3:9-10

Ask for two volunteers to read aloud the first two Bible passages.

1. In the reading from Ezekiel, whose motivation and activity is behind the Hebrew people changing? What do you think might be significant or important about that?

2. What do you think is the difference between a "heart of stone" and a "heart of flesh"?

3. In the reading from Psalm 40, in what ways did God make the writer into a new person?

Ask for two more volunteers to read aloud the passages from John 13 and Colossians 3.

4. When Jesus told his disciples to love one another, that wasn't a radically new commandment—their Jewish faith taught that, too. So what was the new spin that Jesus put on that teaching? (Leader tip: The "newness" was in loving one another the way Jesus had loved.)

5. According to the Colossians reading, how does the old self differ from the new self? What sort of attitudes and activities would you associate with the old self, and which ones would you expect in a new self? (Leader tip: What characteristics of our Creator would be reflected in a new self?)

R and R—Reflect and Respond — 15 minutes

1. With which of the Bible readings do you connect the most? Why?*

2. How would a person "renewed" by God differ from our culture's view of how we should be "new and improved"?

3. Name one way in which you believe God desires for you to change and is at work in you, through the Holy Spirit, to bring about that change.*
   (Leader: Ask group members to make a note of what each person tells about so that group members can encourage one another in working toward these changes.)

Wrap-Up — 2 minutes

Change happens. Change happens around us as well as inside of us, especially during our teenage years. We can choose to look positively at new situations as opportunities for personal growth if we consider that God created us and wants to continually transform us into better human beings.

God desires that we become "new and improved" in our lives and in our faith. And the great news is that God doesn't leave it completely up to us to do the transforming. Rather, the Spirit of God is at work in our lives, shaping us into the people God envisions us and calls us to be—doing God's work, showing God's love, experiencing God's blessings, and giving praise to our God.

Celebrations and Concerns — 10 minutes

Ask group members to tell about something great that has happened recently for which they are thankful. Then invite them to talk about personal concerns or concerns for others they'd like the group to pray for.

Closing Prayer — 10 minutes

Notes

Read aloud or restate in your own words.

What's New?

Life Issue

Leaving behind your childhood and moving toward adulthood

Faith Connection

One step toward a stronger, more mature faith is, ironically, the ability to identify ourselves as children of God and to nurture some of the childlike qualities within us. These qualities include trust, wonder, playfulness, and dependence on God.

Main Ideas

Life used to be so simple and fun—watching cartoons, coloring, playing. Now you have to deal with things like school life, homework, jobs, the social scene, extracurricular activities, planning for life after high school, family stuff, and relationships with friends and others. Many of us wish that, from time to time, we could take a break from our lives and go back to those younger, less stressful days.

But, then again, getting closer to being an adult has its advantages. You have more opportunities to make your own decisions, more freedom to do things with friends. Plus, you can drive, work, and have other responsibilities of your own choosing. This progression toward independence is an exciting and natural one. So too is establishing your own belief system—questioning what you have believed since childhood and trying to figure out what beliefs you can take into adulthood. These are probably beliefs that make sense to you and that you have tested through your own experience.

On your journey to adulthood, keep in mind that becoming an adult—even being a teenager—doesn't mean ridding our lives of everything childish or childlike. The happiest adults and teenagers are those who play, who trust, who look with wonder at simple things (such as bugs) and who depend on their heavenly Parent to protect them, provide for them, direct them, and love them unconditionally.

Jesus loved children. Think about that. He went against the culture of his day (and ours?) by affirming the presence and value of children. He included them. He taught that adults would never understand what he was all about unless they became more childlike. In developing your own faith and growing as a Christian, you'll need to outgrow some *childish* ways and beliefs. But hang on to those *childlike* qualities that will bring a deeper meaning and richer experience to your life and faith.

Read, Research, Reflect — Matthew 18:1-4, 19:13-14, 11:25-26; 1 John 3:1

Read the Scripture passages and the additional info in your *Synago* Notebook. Make notes on the following:

- Who is speaking or telling the story in each passage? Who is the intended audience? What is the context? (What do you think the situation is? What's happening before and after this passage?)
- Pray about and reflect on the reading. What does it say to you?

Memorize

Jesus said, "Let the little children come to me, and do not stop them; for it is to such as these that the kingdom of heaven belongs." (Matthew 19:14, NRSV)

Prepare

- Note your own answers to the questions.
- Get supplies.

Supplies: *Synago* Notebook for each person who doesn't have one (or Bibles or copies of the Bible readings and note cards), pencils or pens.

Opening   5 minutes

Welcome/Announcements/Purpose Statement/Prayer

Warm-Up   5 minutes

What was your favorite toy or "companion" when you were a child?* (blanket, stuffed animal, doll, imaginary person or animal, and so forth)

* Questions with an * should be answered by everyone.

Topic Talk   15 minutes

1. Briefly describe what you were like as a child.*

2. When do you think you stopped being a child?*

3. What are some qualities or characteristics of children that you think people should outgrow as they become adults? Why?

4. What are some qualities of children that people should try to hang onto? Why?

5. What attitudes and behaviors do our society and culture have toward childhood and children?

Word Search   Matthew 18:1-4; 19:13-14; 11:25-26; 1 John 3:1   20 minutes

Ask for a couple of volunteers to read aloud the first two Bible passages.

1. Based on these two readings, what attitude does Jesus seem to have toward children. Does this surprise you? Why, or why not?

2. In what ways is Jesus suggesting that people change to be able to "enter the kingdom of heaven"? What childlike qualities would he want them to have? Why?

Have two more volunteers read aloud the next two passages.

3. In the Matthew 11 reading, what do you think God was keeping "hidden" from the "wise and learned" and revealing instead to children—or those who were average or less sophisticated? Why do you think God would do this?

4. As you understand these last two readings, how would you describe God's attitude toward us and the type of relationship God desires to have with us?

5. Part of 1 John 3:1 says, "The reason the world does not know us [or understand what we're about as Christians] is that it did not know [Jesus]." Do you agree? Why, or why not?

R and R—Reflect and Respond 15 minutes

1. Is it easy or difficult for you to think of yourself as a child of God? Why?*

2. a. Imagine yourself and God as child and parent, and describe your relationship. How would you act toward each other? What would your relationship be like?

   b. How close or far off is this description from the way your relationship with God is right now?

3. What are some childlike qualities that you would like to develop or nurture more within yourself?*

Wrap-Up 2 minutes

Becoming an adult—even being a teenager—doesn't mean ridding our lives of everything childish or childlike. The happiest adults and teenagers are those who play, who trust, who look with wonder at simple things (such as bugs), and who depend on their heavenly Parent to protect them, provide for them, direct them, and love them unconditionally.

Jesus loved children. He went against the culture of his day by affirming their presence and their value. He included them. He taught that adults would never understand what he was all about unless they became more childlike. In developing our own faith and growing as Christians, we'll need to outgrow some *childish* ways and beliefs. But let's hang on to the *childlike* qualities that will bring a deeper meaning and richer experience to our lives and faith.

Celebrations and Concerns 10 minutes

Ask group members to tell something for which they are thankful, then invite them to tell concerns they have about themselves or others for which they would like the group's prayer and support. Encourage group members to write these concerns down and pray for them this week.

Closing Prayer 5 minutes

Invite group members to hold hands. Tell the group that, after you begin the prayer, each person will have a turn to thank God for the person on his or her left, saying a simple, "Thank you, God, for _____." You'll start, then the prayer will go around the circle to the left. When it gets back to you, pray aloud for the concerns the group identified. Then close.

Life Issue

Dealing with stress

Faith Connection

You can trust God to provide for what you truly need, and you can faithfully ask for God's help and peace for those things that worry you.

Main Ideas

"I am so stressed out!" Isn't that a perfect caption for a picture of our society? How often do you feel that way? Too often? Do you ever feel as if you have so much going on that you don't even know where to begin? Does worrying or stressing about something effectively shut you down?

Jesus Christ never promised his followers that their lives would be trouble free. What he told them, however, was that they didn't have to be worriers. They didn't have to be trapped or held down by stress and anxiety. They could trust God to provide for them and to do it beyond measure. Our focus needs to be only on doing what God wants us to do, concentrating on what is truly important in life, such as our relationships with God and others.

Jesus knew that stress and worry don't accomplish or fix anything. They're unhealthy for us too. Being burdened by stress and worry in our lives points to our need for a stronger, more trusting relationship with God. We can honestly tell God about those things that are troubling us. We have available to us, through God's love, a peace that is beyond our understanding. All you have to do is ask.

Read, Research, Reflect   Matthew 6:25-34; John 14:27; Philippians 4:6-7

Read the Scripture passages and the additional info in your *Synago* Notebook. Make notes on the following:

- Who is speaking or telling the story in each passage? Who is the intended audience? What is the context? (What do you think the situation is? What's happening before and after this passage?)
- Pray about and reflect on the reading. What does it say to you?

Memorize

Do not worry about anything, but in everything by prayer and supplication with thanksgiving let your requests be known to God. And the peace of God, which surpasses all understanding, will guard your hearts and your minds in Christ Jesus. (Philippians 4:6-7, NRSV)

Prepare

- Note your own answers to the questions.
- Decide what type of prayer you will use for the closing. (See page 28.)
- Get supplies.

Supplies: *Synago* Notebook for each person who doesn't have one (or Bibles or copies of the Bible readings and note cards), pencils or pens.

* Questions with an * should be answered by everyone.

Opening   5 minutes

Welcome/Announcements/Purpose Statement/Prayer

Warm-Up   5 minutes

Which of these situations would stress you out the most and why? *
  a. baby-sitting five two year olds for ten hours straight
  b. being stuck in an elevator with six other people on the 59th floor for five hours
  c. taking a cross-country trip with your family, by car, for two weeks, with no electronic entertainment
  d. going to school ten hours a day with no summer break

Topic Talk   15 minutes

1. What three things do you think teenagers, in general, stress over the most?

2. Using a scale of 1 to 4, rate yourself as a worrier: *1* for "worry a lot about many things" and *4* for "pretty cool about everything, seldom worry."*

3. What is one major thing that you worry about or that raises your stress level?*

Word Search   15 minutes

Matthew 6:25-34; John 14:27; Philippians 4:6-7

Ask for two volunteers to read aloud Matthew 6:25-34.

1. a. In this reading, what is Jesus telling people not to worry about and why?
    b. What point is he trying to make by talking about birds and flowers?

2. According to Jesus, what should we focus on instead of things like clothes and food? Why?

Have two more volunteers to read aloud the next two passages.

3. In John 14:27, what do you think is the difference between the peace that Jesus says he gives ("my peace") and the kind that the world offers?

4. What is the difference between "do not let your hearts be troubled" and "do not let them be afraid"?

5. In Philippians 4:6, what does Paul encourage us to do in order to experience the incredible peace that God can fill us with? (Leader tip: bring it to God in prayer, in an attitude of thanksgiving, just ask God.)

R&R—Reflect and Respond 15 minutes

1. If Jesus Christ were on your campus and speaking to you and your friends, what would he tell you not to worry about?

2. Can you tell about an experience where you were anxious or worried about something and you experienced the peace of Christ? What was that like?

3. Do you think that Jesus ever got stressed out? What do you think he would do to chill out or to keep from getting worried? (Leader tip: pray, retreat to a place to be alone)

4. What could you say to a friend or do for a friend who was stressed out or worried about something? (Is there someone in our group who needs us to respond this way now?)

Wrap-Up 2 minutes

Jesus Christ never promised his followers that their lives would be trouble free. What he told them, however, was that they didn't have to be worriers. They didn't have to be trapped or held down by stress and worry. They could trust God to provide the things they really needed—and do it beyond measure. The only thing we need to focus on is doing what God wants us to do, concentrating on the really important things in life, like our relationships with God and others.

Jesus knows that stress and worry don't accomplish or fix anything. They're unhealthy for us too. Being burdened by stress and worry in our lives points to our need for a stronger, more trusting relationship with God. We can honestly tell God about those things that are troubling us. We have available to us, through God's love, a peace that is beyond our understanding. All you have to do is ask.

Celebrations and Concerns 10 minutes

Ask group members to tell one thing they're thankful for. After everyone has done this, ask each person to share one thing that they are anxious or worried about. Encourage group members to write these down in their *Synago* Notebooks (or on note cards) and pray for one another's concerns this week.

Closing Prayer 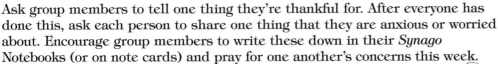 10 minutes

Encourage group members to pray specifically for those worries that were just mentioned. Open the prayer by reading aloud John 14:27 or Philippians 4:6-7.

Read aloud, or restate in your own words, to the group.

Stress-Less

Love Story

Life Issue

Understanding the role of the Bible in the Christian faith

Faith Connection

For Christians, the Bible tells a story. It is the story of God's love for us, of God's desire to be in relationship with us. It is the story of how, throughout the history of God's people and the life of Jesus Christ, God has been calling us into a loving relationship and shaping us into the people God lovingly created us to be.

Main Ideas

The Bible has two parts. The first is the Hebrew Scriptures (the Old Testament or Old Covenant), which tells about Creation, God's covenant with the Hebrew people to be their God, and the lives of men and women used by God to bring about God's plans for the Hebrews. These Scriptures also contain God's Law (the Ten Commandments); songs and other poetic writings; and prophecies warning of the consequences of turning from God, who so passionately loved them.

The second part, the New Testament (or New Covenant), contains stories of the life and teachings of Jesus, who Christians believe fulfilled the Hebrew prophecies of a messiah, or savior who would restore them into a full relationship with God and establish God's kingdom on earth. The New Testament also has stories about people whose worlds were rocked by their encounters with Jesus Christ and who passed on what they understood to be the meaning and implications of his life, teachings, death, resurrection, and the mission of his followers.

But when you get right down to it, the Bible is just a book, although one that has had a greater impact on history and human lives than any ever written. It won't make a difference in your life, however, unless you read it, reflect on it, wrestle with it, and seek to be guided by it. The Bible is a book you can grow with, one that can speak to you at each stage of your life. Though it possesses no magic powers of its own, the Bible—as you discover God's Truth in its pages—can have a powerful effect on your life and faith.

Read, Research, Reflect

2 Peter 1:16-21; John 1:1, 14; Psalm 119:105-112; 2 Timothy 3:16-17

Read the Scripture passages and the additional info in your *Synago* Notebook. Make notes on the following:

- Who is speaking or telling the story in each passage? Who is the intended audience? What is the context? (What do you think the situation is? What's happening before and after this passage?)
- Pray about and reflect on the reading. What does it say to you?

Every part of Scripture is God-breathed and useful one way or another—showing us truth, exposing our rebellion, correcting our mistakes, training us to live God's way. (2 Timothy 3:16, The Message)

Prepare

- Note your own answers to each question.
- Decide how you will close. (See page 28.)
- Get supplies; bring several Bibles with different types of helps in them.

Love Story   Session Plan

Opening   **5 minutes**

Welcome/Announcements/Purpose Statement/Prayer

Warm-Up & Topic Talk   **35 minutes**

Read aloud the following statements about the Bible, and have group members say which one each of them agrees with the most. * (Make sure that everyone feels free to give an honest opinion, with no ridicule from other group members.)

a. The Bible was written by people who tried their best to describe and interpret their understanding of God and God's activity in the world.
b. The Bible was dictated by God without the writers' influence, and everything in it is true.
c. The Bible was inspired by God and recorded by writers who interpreted God's message for their time. It is true in matters of faith and practice, but has historical and scientific errors.
d. The Bible records stories, myths, legends, and contains no more truth than other religious books.

Now compare your group's results to those found in a survey of members of mainline churches.

a. 31% agreed   b. 9% agreed   c. 54% agreed   d. 6% agreed

(Data from "Effective Christian Education: A National Study of Protestant Congregations," by the Search Institute, as reported by L. Benson and Carolyn H. Ecklin, Minneapolis, 1990.)

1. What do you make of these results? Would your friends and parents have similar responses or not? How would most members of your church respond?

2. What have been the biggest influences on you in terms of what you believe about the Bible? *

3. How would you describe your use of the Bible—what you do with it and how often you use it? (such as, rarely use it, occasionally read it, use it for daily devotions, flip through it for a helpful verse when needing guidance, take it to church, and so forth) *

4. Describe your experience with the Bible—has it been positive, frustrating, helpful, a turn-off, interesting, thought-provoking, confusing—what? Why do you think you've had that experience? *

5. Total group effort here—what do group members know about the Bible, such as writers, what's in it, when it was written, how it came to be in its present form, and so on? (Leader tip: You could relate some of the information about the Bible given in the "Main Ideas" section and any other research you've done on it. Also, have the group look through various Bibles to see the types of helps for understanding that are there, including introductions to the books, contents, and any notes.)

Supplies: *Synago* Notebook for each person who doesn't have one (or Bibles or copies of the Bible readings and note cards), pencils or pens, various types of Bibles

* Questions with an * should be answered by everyone.

Word Search **15 minutes**

2 Peter 1:16-21; John 1:1, 14; Psalm 119:105-112; 2 Timothy 3:16-17

Ask volunteers to read aloud 2 Peter 1:16-21 and John 1:1, 14.

1. What can these readings tell us about the people who wrote them?

2. Why do you think they thought it was necessary to include this information about their personal encounter and witness to Jesus Christ?

3. What do verses 20–21 in the Second Peter passage say about the writer's own beliefs about the writing of the Scriptures?

4. Why do you think the writer of John refers to Jesus as the Word? (Sometimes the Bible is referred to as God's Word—think there's any connection?)

Ask volunteers to read aloud the last two passages.

5. What do these readings say are the benefits of knowing the Scriptures?

R&R—Reflect and Respond **10 minutes**

1. What is most difficult for you to believe or understand about the Bible? (How have other group members dealt positively with those same challenges?) *

2. What do you appreciate most, or treasure, about the Bible? *

Wrap-Up **2 minutes**

Read aloud, or restate in your own words.

   Although Christians may disagree as to whether God dictated each word of the Bible and whether everything in it is historically and scientifically accurate, most will agree on these points:
   1. That God inspired the writing, editing, and compilation of the Bible.
   2. That the Bible contains truth about the nature of God and God's plan for the people of God.
   3. That it tells the story of the life and mission of God's son, Jesus Christ.
   4. That it provides instructions for the people of God to live in relationship with God and in community with one another and in the world.

   When you get right down to it, the Bible's just a book, although one that has had a greater impact on history and human lives than any ever written. It won't make a difference in your life, however, unless you read it, reflect on it, wrestle with it, and seek to be guided by it. It's a Book you can grow with, one that can speak to you at each stage of your life. Though it possesses no magic powers of its own, the Bible—as you discover God's Truth in its pages—can have a powerful effect on your life and faith.

Celebrations and Concerns **5 minutes**

Ask group members to share celebrations and concerns.

Closing Prayer **5 minutes**

Life Issue

Feeling left out; reaching out to others

Faith Connection

Christians should invite, accept, and include others, just as Jesus Christ invites and accepts us into relationship with him. Jesus modeled a lifestyle of reaching out to include all people, especially those whom society and the culture excluded.

Main Ideas

Have you ever felt like you were the only one sitting at home on a Friday night, and you were just praying the phone would ring and that a friend—or anybody—would invite you out? Is there a group you'd like to be a part of, but can't seem to get into? Or do you have a pretty tight group of friends who always seem to be doing something together? How open is your group to accepting newcomers, especially people who are different from you?

Most of us tend to see ourselves and others as belonging to one of two groups: insiders and outsiders. You are either in a group or you're not. Feeling like you belong to a group that wants you and accepts you gives an incredible sense of identity and worth. Feeling like a group doesn't want you can be devastating. Why do we place so much importance on being included? It's because God made us to be social beings. It's part of our God-created nature to want to be in relationship with others. We NEED to be in relationship with others.

As Christians, it's not enough to be aware of this aspect of human nature—we must act on it. We have to step outside our "comfort zone" and invite others into our groups. That includes friendship groups as well as youth groups, small groups, churches, and clubs. A first step is to identify who the "outsiders" are in our lives and have compassion for them. (Try imagining how they must feel. Remember times when you felt left out.) The next step is to do something about it. Invite them "in" to your group and shower them with Christian love and acceptance. Be persistent—it shows someone you really do want to include them.

If we faithfully follow the example of Jesus, we will intentionally seek out and hang out with "outsiders." And if you're one of those feeling excluded, take heart in Jesus' genuine love and acceptance of you. Having confidence in being lovable will help give you the confidence to reach out in love to others!

Read, Research, Reflect   Psalm 113:4-8; Mark 2:14-17; Colossians 4:5

Read the Scripture passages and the additional info in your *Synago* Notebook. Make notes on the following:

- Who is speaking or telling the story in each passage? Who is the intended audience? What is the context? (What do you think the situation is? What's happening before and after this passage?)
- Pray about and reflect on the reading. What does it say to you?

Memorize

Be wise in the way you act toward outsiders; make the most of every opportunity. (Colossians 4:5, NIV)

Prepare

- Note your own answers to each question.
- Decide what type of prayer you will use for the closing. (See page 28.)
- Get supplies.

The Outsiders   Session Plan

Supplies: *Synago* Notebook for each person who doesn't have one (or Bibles or copies of the Bible readings and note cards), pencils or pens

*Questions with an * should be answered by everyone.*

Opening   5 minutes

Welcome/Announcements/Purpose Statement/Prayer

Warm-Up   3 minutes

In three minutes, brainstorm as many groups or clubs as you can that a teenager can belong to? (Leader: watch the clock and keep count of how many things the group comes up with.)

Topic Talk   15 minutes

1. a. What groups or individuals at school would you describe as "outsiders"?
   b. What identifies them as outsiders?

2. What groups or individuals in your community would you identify as "outsiders"—not socially acceptable, intentionally left out, or actively excluded?

3. Think about a time when you felt left out. Tell the group about it. *

Word Search   Psalm 113:4-8; Mark 2:14-17; Colossians 4:5   20 minutes

Ask a volunteer to read aloud Psalm 113:4-8.

1. a. Who would be the insiders and outsiders in this reading?
   b. In what ways do the rich and poor continue to be insiders and outsiders today?
   c. In the reading, what action does God take with the poor and the powerful?

Have another volunteer read aloud Mark 2:14-17.

2. Who were the insiders and outsiders in this reading, and why?

3. Why do you think this story is included in the Bible? What does it tell you about Jesus Christ?

4. How do you think the tax collectors and other designated "sinners" felt when Jesus ate with them? (To eat with someone was a sign of friendship. It still is, isn't it?)

Ask a volunteer to read aloud Colossians 4:5.

5. In this context, "outsiders" were persons who were outside the Christian faith. Why do you think the Apostle Paul thought it necessary to give this advice to some early Christians?

6. How does Paul's advice relate to us and our friends and acquaintances?

R&R—Reflect and Respond 5 minutes

1. If God were hosting a dinner in your community, who would be seated together at the table?

2. If Jesus were hanging out during lunch time at your school, with whom would he be eating? Are there specific tables where he would sit?

3. How inviting and accepting is our small group? In what ways, as a small group, are we being Christlike with outsiders? How can we be more invitational and accepting of others? (Be really honest here.)

4. Take a moment to think of one person "outside" your small group, youth group, or peer group, whom you can befriend. Share that person's first name with the group. By sharing these names, we can hold each other accountable to follow through on reaching out to include them.

Wrap-Up 2 minutes

Most of us tend to see ourselves and others as belonging to one of two groups: insiders and outsiders. You are either in a group or you're not. Feeling like you belong to a group that wants you and accepts you can give you an incredible sense of identity and worth. Feeling like a group doesn't want you can be devastating. Why do we place so much importance on being included? It's because God made us to be social beings. It's part of our God-created nature to want to be in relationship with others. We NEED to be in relationship with others.

As Christians, it's not enough just to be aware of this social aspect of human nature—we must act on it. We have to step outside our "comfort zone" and invite others into our groups. That includes friendship groups as well as youth groups, small groups, churches, and clubs. A first step is to identify who the "outsiders" are in our lives and have compassion for them. (Try imagining how they must feel. Remember times when you felt left out.) The next step is to do something about it—invite them "in" to your group and show them Christian love and acceptance. Be persistent. This shows someone you really do want to include them.

If we faithfully follow the example of Jesus, we will intentionally seek out and hang out with "outsiders." And if you're one of those feeling excluded, take heart in Jesus' genuine love and acceptance of you. Having confidence in being lovable can give you the confidence to reach out in love to others!

Read aloud, or restate in your own words, to the group.

Celebrations and Concerns 15 minutes

Ask group members to share recent celebrations and prayer requests for themselves or others.

Closing Prayer 5-10 minutes

Encourage group members to pray for each other's concerns and to name a person God is leading them to reach out to and invite to the small group. (Leader: Write down these names and follow up with your group members during the week.)

The Outsiders

Life Issue

How to pray

Faith Connection

Prayer is one of the most important disciplines of the Christian faith. It connects us with our Creator God, with our brothers and sisters in the faith, and with our needful world. Jesus prayed faithfully and taught his disciples to pray too.

Main Ideas

Let's talk about your prayer life. Do you pray often? on a regular basis? Do you have a special time and place for prayer? Are you comfortable praying aloud in front of others? Is prayer a meaningful time for you? Do you wish you prayed more? wish you prayed longer? wish you heard God talk back? wish you didn't fall asleep sometimes? What would you like to change about your prayer life? Do you believe God hears and answers your prayers? What do you pray for? Why do you pray?

For Christians, we need prayer like we need oxygen. Prayer keeps us spiritually alive as it keeps us in touch with our loving Creator God. Some Christians struggle with prayer, getting hung up on saying the "right" words and praying for the "right" things. Prayer is just our honest dialogue with God. In prayer, we talk intimately with God as we would a loving Parent, who is there to care for us, provide for us, and sometimes just listen to us. It's not your words that are important, as much as acknowledging your need for God—whether you're reaching out, crying out, or even lashing out. God desires a relationship with you; and the quality, depth, and intensity of that relationship—like any relationship—hinges on communication. In a relationship with God, that's prayer.

There is no special formula when it comes to praying, although the Bible has some guidelines that can help you develop a well-rounded and grounded prayer life. The key is to just pray—honestly, regularly, confidently. Prayer makes a difference.

Read, Research, Reflect   Luke 11:1-4; Matthew 6:5-8; 1 Thessalonians 5:16-18

Read the Scripture passages and the additional info in your *Synago* Notebook. Make notes on the following:

- Who is speaking or telling the story in each passage? Who is the intended audience? What is the context? (What do you think the situation is? What's happening before and after this passage?)
- Pray about and reflect on the reading. What does it say to you?

Memorize

So Jesus told them, "Pray in this way: 'Father, help us to honor your name. Come and set up your kingdom. Give us each day the food we need. Forgive our sins, as we forgive everyone who has done wrong to us. And keep us from being tempted.'"
(Luke 11:2-4, CEV)

Prepare

- Note your own answers to each question.
- Get supplies.
- Become familiar with the ACTS method of prayer, described in the Closing Prayer.

Opening

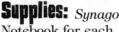 **5 minutes**

Welcome/Announcements/Purpose Statement/Prayer

Warm-Up

5 minutes

What's the most outrageous thing you ever prayed for? How was your prayer "answered"? *

Topic Talk

 10 minutes

1. What do you find most challenging when it comes to your own prayer life? (example, finding time to pray, knowing what to say, distractions) *

2. What different kinds or types of prayers can you think of? (Leader tip: such as, a sentence prayer, breath prayer, prayer of confession, prayer of thanks, blessing, grace at meal, and so on)

3. Share a time when you had a very meaningful prayer experience. What do you think made it special?

Word Search

20 minutes

 Luke 11:1-4; Matthew 6:5-8; 1 Thessalonians 5:16-18

Ask for a volunteer to read aloud the passage from Luke.

1. How does it make you feel knowing that Jesus' disciples asked to be taught how to pray? Why do you think they asked Jesus that?

2. a. What suggestions did Jesus have for praying?
   b. Take each of his suggestions and give a specific example of what you might say in your own words.

Ask another volunteer to read aloud the passage from Matthew.

3. What point is Jesus making here about what really matters when you pray? Give a current example of what he's talking about.

4. Do you think Jesus is suggesting we should never pray in front of other people? Why or why not?

5. If God knows what you're going to ask for, then why should you pray for it?

Ask for a volunteer to read aloud the last passage.

6. What could Paul be talking about when he says to "pray without ceasing"?

Supplies: *Synago* Notebook for each person who doesn't have one (or Bibles or copies of the Bible readings and note cards), pencils or pens

* *Questions with an * should be answered by everyone.*

Notes

R&R—Reflect and Respond 15 minutes

1. What specific suggestions or words of encouragement do you think Jesus would offer you to strengthen or enrich your personal prayer life? *

2. Pick one thing to work on during the week to improve your prayer life and make it a regular part of your routine, such as setting aside a certain time each day to pray, spending some of your prayer time in silence, keeping a daily journal of your prayers, being aware of talking to God throughout your day. Tell the group what you're going to work on (Leader: write it down), so they can hold you to it and encourage you. *

Wrap-Up 2 minutes

Read aloud, or restate in your own words.

For Christians, we need prayer like we need oxygen. Prayer keeps us spiritually alive as it keeps us in touch with our loving Creator God. Prayer is just our honest dialogue with God. In prayer, we talk intimately with God as we would a loving Parent, who is there to care for us, provide for us, and sometimes just listen to us. It's not your words that are important, as much as acknowledging your need for God—whether you're reaching out, crying out, or even lashing out. God desires a relationship with you, and the quality, depth, and intensity of that relationship—like any relationship—hinges on communication. In a relationship with God, that's prayer. The key is to just pray—honestly, regularly, confidently. It will make a difference.

Celebrations and Concerns 10 minutes

Ask group members to share something great that's happened in their lives recently and something for which they would like prayer.

Closing Prayer 15 minutes

Explain how to pray using the "ACTS of prayer" method; remind the group that this is just one way—it is not the only way to pray:

A is for words of **adoration** to God. Adoration is basically paying compliments to God or making adoring statements about God, such as, "God, you are so loving"; "God, you are awesome"; "O God, your love and mercy and understanding are beyond our understanding." (Leader tip: Many people find adoration challenging because it's easily confused with being thankful, so give examples.)

C is for **confession**—confessing our sins to God, either our personal sins ("forgive me for lying to my mom") or our collective sins ("forgive us for being apathetic to the pain and the injustices around us at school").

T is for **thanksgiving**. You know how to do that.

S is for **special requests**. (Some folks say "supplication.") This would be prayer requests for yourself or for others, such as helping you to forgive a friend or for the healing of a sick grandparent.

Invite the group to close in prayer using the ACTS of prayer. Starting with A, go around the circle with group members saying one phrase or sentence complimenting God's character or activity. Then go around a second time, with group members confessing one thing for which they desire God's forgiveness. Then go around again, this time doing the T— thanksgiving. End by going around the circle a final time, with each group member praying specifically for a personal need or for others.

Synago: Light in the Dark

Life Issue

Needing guidance in making important decisions

Faith Connection

God helps and guides us in making decisions through Scripture, through the support of Christian friends and our faith community, through the Holy Spirit within us, and through other ways and means (such as people and experiences) that God may use in our lives.

Main Ideas

One thing you can be certain about in life is that you will always be making decisions. As you get older, not only do you have more decisions to make, but they also get more complicated. The results of your decisions seem to have more profound and lasting effects on your life. The stakes get higher. Making decisions becomes a bigger and bigger deal.

Even though you are often perfectly capable of making your own decisions, at times you will want to seek direction in order to make the best decisions. How can you be sure whether your sources of information are accurate? (You should be careful about information from peers, the media, and the Internet, among other sources.)

Christians have a wealth of resources available to guide them in making good decisions, decisions that seek to honor God and acknowledge Jesus' lordship in their lives. You may already be using some of the helps God provides for you to make faithful decisions. They include Scripture, prayer, parents, Christian friends, a supportive faith community (such as church or small group), and meaningful experiences and insight that God gives you through the Holy Spirit.

Any decision you make is important to God. Don't be hesitant about asking for directions. Be open to the direction that God can give you, in whatever form that may take and wherever it may lead.

Read, Research, Reflect
Proverbs 3:5-6; Psalm 119:97-104

Read the Scripture passages and the additional info in your *Synago* Notebook. Make notes on the following:

- Who is speaking or telling the story in each passage? Who is the intended audience? What is the context? (What do you think the situation is? What's happening before and after this passage?)
- Pray about and reflect on the reading. What does it say to you?

Memorize

Trust in the LORD with all your heart, and do not rely on your own insight. In all your ways acknowledge him, and he will make straight your paths. (Proverbs 3:5-6, NRSV)

Prepare

- Note your own answers to each question.
- Decide how you'll close in prayer. (See page 28.)
- Get supplies.

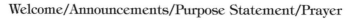

Getting Directions

Session Plan

Supplies: *Synago* Notebook for each person who doesn't have one (or Bibles or copies of the Bible readings and note cards), pencils or pens

* Questions with an * should be answered by everyone.

Opening

5 minutes

Welcome/Announcements/Purpose Statement/Prayer

Warm-Up

5 minutes

If you were camping and got lost in the woods, which of the following would be most helpful to you in getting back to the camp site? *
  a. a compass
  b. a topographic map of the area
  c. the trail of food crumbs you probably left behind
  d. staying put and periodically yelling for help
  e. you wouldn't get lost to begin with—you have a great sense of direction

Topic Talk

10 minutes

1. If you can, tell a story about being lost and whether or not you or someone you were with asked for directions. (lost driving, in a building, in a park, wherever)

2. Are you better at giving direction (advice) or taking direction (advice)? *

3. Where or to whom do you go for advice? Whom do you trust the most to help you with a decision? *

Word Search   Proverbs 3:5-6; Psalm 119:97-104

15 minutes

Ask for two volunteers to read aloud the Bible passages.

1. a. In Proverbs 3:5-6, what do you think it means when it says "[the Lord] will make straight your paths"?
   b. In what ways might God do this?

2. What three things are we encouraged to do so that we have God's guidance?

3. According to Psalm 119, in what ways does the writer get direction from God's Word?

R&R—Reflect and Respond

1. Why can it be difficult to "trust in the Lord with all your heart"?

2. Why might relying in your own insight not help you make the best decisions?

3. What does it mean to acknowledge God in all the decisions we make? How can we do that?

4. Can you think of a time when you needed direction in your life, and God provided it for you? How did you experience God's direction?

5. Think of an area in your life or a decision you're facing for which you need direction. Tell the group about it. (Group members can respond, as they feel led, to provide direction, support, and encouragement.) *

Wrap-Up

2 minutes

Even though you are often perfectly capable of making your own decisions, at times you will want to seek direction in order to make the best decisions. Christians have a wealth of resources available to guide them in making good decisions, decisions that seek to honor God and acknowledge Jesus' lordship in their lives. You may already be using some of the helps God provides for you to make faithful decisions. They include Scripture, prayer, parents, Christian friends, a supportive faith community (such as church or small group), and meaningful experiences and insight that God gives you through the Holy Spirit.

Any decision you make is important to God. Don't be hesitant about asking for directions. Be open to the direction that God can give you, in whatever form that may take and wherever it may lead.

Celebrations and Concerns

10 minutes

Ask group members to share things they're thankful for, then invite them to make prayer requests for themselves or others.

Closing Prayer

5 minutes

Invite group members during the closing prayer to give thanks to God, to pray for one another's concerns, and to pray for those situations in which they need God's direction.

Notes

Read aloud, or restate in your own words, to the group.

Getting Directions

Life Issue

What makes a good friend

Faith Connection

A Christian friend cares for the spiritual, as well as the physical, well-being of his or her friends.

Main Ideas

What kind of a friend are you? No, what kind of a friend are you, really? Are you trustworthy? Loyal? Dependable? Do you truly care about the health and well-being of your friends? Do you discourage them from doing things that could harm them or get them in trouble? What lengths would you be willing to go in order to help a friend? Are you the kind of friend that you would like to have?

Friendships are very important, but often very fragile, when we're teenagers. It's great when you have one or two best friends—not so great when you don't, but wish you did. You may also be discovering that you've drifted in and out of some friendships from middle school and high school, made some new ones, and totally dropped some. You're also in the process of exploring and determining what you really want in a friendship and who your real friends are.

Some people toss the term *friend* around pretty casually. They may say someone is their friend, but the way they treat them says otherwise. Does a friend encourage you to do something that might hurt you or get you into trouble? Does a friend take advantage of you? Does a friend lie to you? Does a friend talk about you behind your back? Does a friend not care what happens to you? Does a friend let you take the blame for something he or she did? Although the answer may seem obvious, you can probably think of people who do those things to people they call their "friends."

The Bible offers several examples of true friendship. Not only do Christians care about the physical well-being of a friend, they care about that friend's spiritual health too. If you are a Christian and you know the joy of being forgiven and accepted and loved unconditionally, the joy of being a child of God and of being in a relationship with Jesus Christ, then you want the people you love to know that joy as well. Invite Christ to be at the heart of your friendships. Loving someone with Christ's love will be a life-changing experience, for both of you.

Read, Research, Reflect

Luke 5:17-26

Read the Scripture passages and the additional info in your *Synago* Notebook. Make notes on the following:

- Who is speaking or telling the story in each passage? Who is the intended audience? What is the context? (What do you think the situation is? What's happening before and after this passage?)
- Pray about and reflect on the reading. What does it say to you?

Memorize

When Jesus saw [the friends'] faith, he said, "Friend, your sins are forgiven." (Luke 5:20, NIV)

Prepare

- Note your own answers to each question.
- Decide how you will close in prayer, if you don't use the suggested closing. (See page 28.)
- Get supplies. Don't forget what you need for the friendship bracelets.

What Are Friends For?

Opening

5 minutes

Welcome/Announcements/Purpose Statement/Prayer

Warm-Up

3 minutes

Have the group brainstorm as many famous pairs of friends (from real life, cartoons, TV series, and so forth) as they can think of, while you write them down. Count how many you come up with.

Topic Talk
15 minutes

1. What are the qualities of a good friend? Everyone should come up with at least one. *

2. What is the difference between a true friend and someone who just calls you a friend?

3. What is the best thing that a friend has ever done for you—something that showed true friendship? *

4. What role does your faith play in your friendships?

Word Search   Luke 5:17-26

20 minutes

Have volunteers read aloud the passage.

1. Who are the main characters in this story? What are they doing there?

2. Compare why the Pharisees and teachers of the law were there to why the men carrying their paralyzed friend were there.

3. What do you imagine the men had to go through to get their friend in front of Jesus? (Leader tip: Probably carrying him all over town then up to the roof, tearing out a hole in the roof, finding some way to lower him)

4. On the basis of whose faith was the paralyzed man forgiven?

5. Why did Jesus first tell the man that his sins were forgiven, instead of telling him to get up and walk? (Leader tip: Jesus knew the Pharisees and their buds were trying to set him up in a theological debate; he wanted to make it clear to them, in public, that he knew what they were up to and that his authority came from God.)

6. a. What did the paralyzed man experience as a result of his encounter with Jesus Christ?
   b. What did the others who were there experience?
   c. What did they do in response to what they saw?

Supplies: lengths of twine, ribbon, leather, or cloth for friendship bracelets (one for each group member, plus extra lengths for visitors); *Synago* Notebook for each person who doesn't have one (or Bibles or copies of the Bible readings and note cards); pencils or pens

* Questions with an * should be answered by everyone.

R&R—Reflect and Respond 20 minutes

1. What can we learn about being a good friend, from the friends of the paralyzed man?

2. Do you find talking with your friends about your faith easy or difficult? * Why?

3. Has someone in your life been a true friend? In what way? Any friends who helped you grow closer to God and Jesus Christ or helped you to heal in other ways?

4. Think silently for a moment about a friend of yours who needs, in some way, the healing touch of Christ, whether physically, emotionally, or spiritually. (Hand out a friendship bracelet to each person.) Give this bracelet to your friend sometime this week as a token of your friendship and of your personal commitment to being a good friend to this person, to love him or her with Christ's love, and to pray for him or her.

Wrap-Up 2 minutes

Read aloud, or restate in your own words.

   Friendships are very important, but often very fragile, when we're teenagers. You may also be discovering that you've drifted in and out of some friendships from middle school and high school, made some new ones, and totally dropped some. You're also in the process of exploring and determining what you really want in a friendship and who your real friends are.

   Some people toss the term *friend* around pretty casually. They may say someone is their friend, but their actions say otherwise. The way you treat a friend speaks volumes about how you really feel towards that person and whether or not you value him or her.

   The Bible offers several examples of true friendship. Not only do Christians care about the physical well-being of a friend, they care about that friend's spiritual health too. If you are a Christian and you know the joy of being forgiven and loved unconditionally, then you want the people you love to know that joy as well. Invite Christ to be at the heart of your friendships. Loving someone with Christ's love will be a life-changing experience, for both of you.

Celebrations and Concerns 10 minutes

Ask group members to tell any celebrations they have, then concerns for themselves and others. Encourage group members to be in prayer during the week for those concerns.

Closing Prayer 5 minutes

Close with a breath prayer. Go around once, with each group member saying the first name of a friend or two for whom he or she is thankful. Go around a second time, saying the first name of the friend in need of Christ's healing love who will be given the friendship bracelet.

Thirst Quencher Leader Prep

Life Issue

Feeling spiritually dry or empty

Faith Connection

Just as in any relationship, there will be times when we feel tight with God and times when we feel distant. We can trust God, however, to respond to our spiritual yearnings.

Main Ideas

No matter how much love and commitment you have in a relationship, you will have good days and bad days. Days when you feel really connected and close, and days when you feel rejected, lonely, deserted. You experience that in a relationship with God too. The Bible is filled with stories of people who experienced frustrating spiritually-dry spells and then closeness and intimacy with God, as well.

Sometimes we experience spiritual "thirst" after we have had an intense, "mountain-top" faith experience and then return to "normal" life; sometimes we set ourselves up for a dry spell by pulling away from God and not spending time in prayer, worship, Christian fellowship, or reflecting on God's Word. Sometimes it seems you get dumped on from all sides—all sorts of bad stuff happens at once, almost more than you can take, and you wonder, "Where is God?"

The writer of Psalm 42 was going through something like that, but what kept him going was recalling those times he had experienced God's presence. He knew that he could count on that happening again, because he believed in a God that would not let him down or desert him. He trusted in God's love for him and in their relationship, knowing that, in time, his thirst for God's presence would be quenched.

Like the psalmist, we can also take heart that our dry times are only temporary. But when they come—and they will—just keep an honest dialogue going with God, telling God how it is with you and how much you desire to feel that closeness again. It is God's desire too.

Read, Research, Reflect

Psalm 42

Read the Scripture passages and the additional info in your *Synago* Notebook. Make notes on the following:

- Who is speaking or telling the story in each passage? Who is the intended audience? What is the context? (What do you think the situation is? What's happening before and after this passage?)
- Pray about and reflect on the reading. What does it say to you?

Memorize

As the deer longs for flowing streams, so my soul longs for you, O God. My soul thirsts for God, for the living God. (Psalm 42:1-2. NRSV)

Prepare

- Note your own answers to the Session questions.
- Decide how you'll close in prayer. (See page 28.)
- Get supplies.

Supplies: *Synago* Notebook for each person, pencils or pens, Bibles or copies of the Bible readings and note cards for those who don't have a *Synago* Notebook

Opening　　　　**5 minutes**

Welcome/Announcements /Purpose Statement/Prayer

Warm-Up　　　　**5 minutes**

If you were really thirsty, what type of drink would you choose to quench your thirst? Why that one instead of the other possible choices? *

* Questions with an * should be answered by everyone.

Topic Talk　　　　**15 minutes**

1. Briefly describe a time when you were extremely thirsty or hungry. How did you cope, and how did you eventually satisfy your thirst or hunger? *

2. What are some other things, besides physical needs for food and drink, that teenagers long for or really want?

3. What about spiritual hunger or thirst? How do teenagers experience that, and what do they do to satisfy it? *

Word Search　　　**Psalm 42**　　　**20 minutes**

Ask volunteers to read Psalm 42 (the NRSV translation). Then ask group members to listen and follow along silently as you read it aloud again, this time using *The Message*.

1. What is the writer of these verses longing for?

2. To what does he compare his longing for God?

3. How would you describe the writer's mood and situation? What seems to have happened to him?

4. Why do you think people are asking him, "Where is your God?"

5. What are some specific things the writer focuses on to give himself hope? (Leader tip: an awesome worship experience he had, experiences of God's presence in nature, remembering God's daily presence with him)

R&R—Reflect and Respond　　　**20 minutes**

1. Do you ever feel like the writer of this psalm? What expressions or phrases do you connect with the most? *

2. We have all experienced spiritual dryness or emptiness at some time in our lives. Maybe some of us are even going through a period like that now. Tell the group about an experience you have had of being spiritually dry. What do you think caused it and what was it like? How did it go away? *

3. Why do you think we go through periods of feeling close to God and periods of feeling distant from God? Why can't we always have those confident, "mountain-top" feelings of faith?

4. When the psalm writer was feeling down, he made himself think about those times when he was experiencing the presence of God. If you were spiritually dry, is there a specific time you would think about to remember feeling close to God? Tell us about it. *

5. When we find ourselves feeling spiritually dry, what are some specific things we can do to help quench our thirst? (Leader tip: prayer, writing a letter to God, finding a natural setting or place where we can focus on God, reading the Bible, talking to or praying with a Christian friend, being in service or mission to others, listening to music that focuses our thoughts on God, recalling God's blessings and activity in our lives, journaling)

Wrap-Up 2 minutes

Read aloud, or restate in your own words.

No matter how much love and commitment you have in a relationship, there are going to be good days and bad days. Days when you feel really connected and close, and days when you feel rejected, lonely, deserted. You experience that in a relationship with God too. The Bible is filled with stories of people who experienced frustrating spiritual dry spells and closeness and intimacy with God, as well. Sometimes we experience spiritual "thirst" after we've had an intense, "mountain top" faith experience and then return to "normal" life; sometimes we set ourselves up for a dry spell by pulling away from God and not spending time in prayer, worship, Christian fellowship, or reflecting on God's Word. Sometimes it seems you get dumped on from all sides—all sorts of bad stuff happens at once, almost more than you can take, and you wonder, "Where is God?"

The writer of Psalm 42 was going through something like that, but what kept him going was recalling those times he had experienced God's presence. He knew that he could count on that happening again, because he believed in a God that would not let him down or desert him. He trusted in God's love for him and in their relationship, knowing that, in time, his thirst for God's presence would be quenched. Like the psalmist, we can also take heart that our dry times are only temporary. But when they come—and they will—just keep an honest dialogue going with God, telling God how it is with you and how much you desire to feel that closeness again. It is God's desire too.

Celebrations and Concerns 5 minutes

Ask group members to share any celebrations they have, then concerns for themselves and others.

Closing Prayer 5 minutes

Have group members hold hands during the prayer. End the prayer time by reading aloud Psalm 42:11: "Why are you cast down, O my soul, and why are you disquieted within me? Hope in God; for I shall again praise him, my help and my God."

Thirst Quencher

Serve It Up

Leader Prep

Life Issue

Serving others; focusing on the needs of others rather than our own desires.

Faith Connection

Jesus Christ called his disciples to follow him. The example he set for them—and for us—was one of serving others. As his followers, we are also called by Jesus, and empowered by the Holy Spirit, to put aside our expectations to be the one served and, instead, to meet the needs of others.

Main Ideas

What gives meaning to your life? Sports? Academic achievements? Music? Exploring the outdoors? Working? Having a loving family or a special group of friends? Service to others? If you've had the opportunity to be in service to others, you might agree that serving others can bring an incredible amount of meaning, purpose, and fulfillment to your life.

When you live in a culture that promotes a "Me-First, Me-Get-Best, Me-Get-Most" philosophy, it's easy to become shallow and self-centered. Focusing on yourself—giving what you want priority over everything and everybody else—distracts you from activities and a way of life that will bring you more satisfaction than you can imagine.

It is ironic that helping others and, seemingly, getting nothing out of it for yourself is what truly makes you feel good inside and gives your life a sense of purpose and meaning. That's because when we make choices to serve the needs of others, we are fulfilling God's purpose for us—to be channels of God's love and caring.

Jesus Christ is our ultimate example for serving others. Even though he was the son of God, he didn't consider himself better than others. Comforting the poor, healing the sick, or even washing the dirty feet of his friends wasn't beneath him.

As his disciples, we take up where Jesus left off. So many people need our time, our help, our attention, our resources, our love. Make a personal commitment to live a life of serving those in need—in big ways and little ways, at home and in far away places, all by yourself or with others, in secret and with lots of attention. When you serve up God's love to others, you will feel the touch of God yourself.

Read, Research, Reflect
Micah 6:8; Luke 22:27; Philippians 2:1-4

Read the Scripture passages and the additional info in your *Synago* Notebook. Make notes on the following:

- Who is speaking or telling the story in each passage? Who is the intended audience? What is the context? (What do you think the situation is? What's happening before and after this passage?)
- Pray about and reflect on the reading. What does it say to you?

Memorize

Put yourself aside, and help others get ahead. . . . Forget yourselves long enough to lend a helping hand. (Philippians 2:4, Message)

Prepare

- Note your own answers to the session questions.
- Decide how you'll close in prayer. (See page 28.)
- Get supplies.

60

Synago: Light in the Dark

Serve It Up

Session Plan

Supplies: *Synago* Notebook for each person, pencils or pens, Bibles or copies of the Bible readings and note cards for those who don't have a *Synago* Notebook

Opening

5 minutes

Welcome/Announcements/Purpose Statement/Prayer

Warm-Up

5 minutes

Briefly describe the worst service you ever got at a restaurant or store, or a recent experience of poor service. *

Topic Talk

10 minutes

1. On a scale of one to six—one being "self-obsessed" and six being "exclusively focused on others"—rate where you think the average senior high student falls. *

2. Does our society and culture seem to pull teenagers toward one end of the scale or the other? Explain.

3. What or who has made a significant impact on the extent to which you focus more on yourself or others? Explain. * (friends, church, youth group, parents, a personal experience, other important adults, and so forth)

* Questions with an * should be answered by everyone.

Word Search   Micah 6:8; Mark 10:45; Philippians 2:3-4
15 minutes

Ask a volunteer to read Micah 6:8.

1. How does someone "do justice"?

2. What do you think it means to "walk humbly" with God?

3. If you lived by this verse for the next month, how might your life be different? What changes in your attitudes, routine, and lifestyle would you need to make to live by this verse?

Ask another volunteer to read the verses from Mark and Philippians.

4. a. According to these two readings, what are the characteristics of the life of a Christian?
   b. What would be an example of Philippians 2:4, of putting yourself aside and helping others get ahead?

R&R—Reflect and Respond

25 minutes

1. Think about the lifestyle that Jesus Christ's disciples are to have, as described in these readings. According to these passages, what is a primary indicator of someone's faithfulness to the Christian life?

2. Do these Bible readings, with their emphasis on service-oriented lives, support or challenge your understanding of what it means to be a Christian? Explain. *

3. What challenges or roadblocks are there to living a life of service to the needy? (For example, selfishness, finding opportunities to help others, attitude that someone else will do it)

   Who are "the needy" in our lives and in our world?

4. What is one thing you could do to more faithful in serving the needs of others? *

5. Consider a way that this group could more faithfully follow Christ by serving others. Plan it and do it. (Leader: Encourage your group to do something that puts your group in personal contact with persons in need, rather than just raising money.)

Read aloud, or restate in your own words.

Wrap-Up

2 minutes

When you live in a culture that promotes a "Me-First, Me-Get-Best, Me-Get-Most" philosophy, it's easy to become shallow and self-centered. Focusing on yourself—giving what you want priority over everything and everybody else—distracts you from activities and a way of life that will bring you more real satisfaction than you can imagine.

It is ironic that helping others and, seemingly, getting nothing out of it for yourself is what truly makes you feel good inside. It gives our lives a sense of purpose and meaning. That's because when we make choices to serve the needs of others, then we are fulfilling God's purpose for us—to be channels of God's love and caring.

Jesus Christ is our ultimate example for serving others. Even though he was the son of God, he never considered himself better than others. It was never beneath him—or an inconvenience—to comfort the poor, heal the sick, or even wash the dirty feet of his friends.

As his disciples, we take up where Jesus left off. So many people need our time, our help, our attention, our resources, our love. Make a personal commitment to live a life of serving those in need—in big ways and little ways, at home and in far away places, all by yourself or with others, in secret and with lots of attention. When you serve up God's love to others, you will feel the touch of God yourself.

Celebrations and Concerns

5 minutes

Invite group members to share celebrations and concerns.

Closing Prayer

5 minutes

Synago: Light in the Dark

Life Issue

Experiencing hurt and suffering

Faith Connection

God reaches out to those who are hurting and suffering. Although we may never understand why bad things happen that cause us pain, we can be sure that God wants to comfort us, give us strength, and heal the hurt.

Main Ideas

Sometimes life hurts. Although folks will tell you that your teenage years are supposed to be the best, they seem to be peppered with tragedies that surprise you and wipe you out—mentally, emotionally, spiritually. Parents separate or divorce. A best friend moves away. A family member or friend has a terminal illness. Someone you care about dies.

During times of pain and loss, you may want to blame God or get angry at God. You may want to toss out this God-and-faith-stuff altogether. Or, you may have some of the greatest faith experiences of your life, as you discover God at work within tragedy, and as you and others experience God's comfort, peace, strength, and healing in times of great sorrow.

As a Christian, not only can you experience God's peace and comfort when you hurt, but you can also be a channel of that peace and comfort to others who are hurting. It may be through your response to them in their time of suffering, that they experience the love of God that will help to ease their pain and heal their hurt.

Read, Research, Reflect   Matthew 5:4; 2 Corinthians 1:3-4; Romans 8:28

Read the Scripture passages and the additional info in your *Synago* Notebook. Make notes on the following:

- Who is speaking or telling the story in each passage? Who is the intended audience? What is the context? (What do you think the situation is? What's happening before and after this passage?)
- Pray about and reflect on the reading. What does it say to you?

Memorize

"Blessed are those who mourn, for they will be comforted." (Matthew 5:4)

Prepare

- Note your own answers to the questions.
- Decide how you'll close in prayer. (See page 28.)
- Get supplies; don't forget the tissues.

Supplies: Box of tissues, *Synago* Notebook for each person, pencils or pens, Bibles or copies of the Bible readings and note cards for those who don't have a *Synago* Notebook

Opening

5 minutes

Welcome/Announcements/Purpose Statement/Prayer

Warm-Up
5 minutes

We're going to have a "Show and Tell" time with scars. If you have a scar, briefly tell us how you got it. Show it to us, if it's not in too personal a place. If you don't have a scar, briefly tell us about the worst injury or illness you ever had.*

Topic Talk
10 minutes

1. Do you think teenagers today experience more emotional pain and hurt than their parents did as teenagers? Why or why not?

2. What are some of the ways that teenagers deal with pain, loss, or hurt in their lives?

3. How do you personally deal with pain in your life? * (For example, spend time alone, cry, keep it inside, talk to others, pray, get moody, work out, try to numb it or escape through drugs/alcohol, other distractions)

* Questions with an * should be answered by everyone.

Word Search   Matthew 5:4; 2 Corinthians 1:3-4; Romans 8:28
15 minutes

Ask volunteers to read the passages.

1. According to these Scripture readings, how does God want to respond to us when we are in pain? What do you think that reveals about the nature of God?

2. In Matthew 5:4, what do you think it means by "blessed are those who mourn"?

3. According to the verses in 2 Corinthians, what happens as a result of God showing us compassion and comforting us during difficult times?

4. What does Romans 8:28 say about God's activity in our lives?

R&R—Reflect and Respond

25 minutes

1. How can Romans 8:28 affect the way we look at and deal with painful events?

2. If you can, give an example of how you have experienced or witnessed God working "for the good" in a tragic situation.

3. Tell about a time or event in your life that was or is very painful. Have you been able to see God at work through it in any way? If so, how? If you haven't, feel free to be honest about that, too. * (Leader: Remind everyone of the confidential nature of the small group—What's said here, stays here. Make sure you and other group members give full attention to whomever is sharing. Respond lovingly with a compassionate word, pat on the shoulder, or hug—whatever is appropriate— to those who may need comfort. Have a box of tissues nearby.)

4. What are some specific ways that you can lovingly respond to someone who is going through a painful time? In what ways can you be a channel of God's love and comfort?

Wrap-Up 2 minutes

Read aloud, or restate in your own words.

Sometimes life hurts. Although folks will tell you that your teenage years are supposed to be the best, they seem to be peppered with tragedies that surprise you and wipe you out—mentally, emotionally, spiritually. Parents separate or divorce. A best friend moves away. A family member or friend has a terminal illness. Someone you care about dies.

During times of pain and loss, you may want to blame God or get angry at God. You may want to toss out this God-and-faith-stuff altogether. Or, you may have some of the greatest faith experiences of your life, as you discover God at work within tragedy, and as you and others experience God's comfort, peace, strength, and healing in times of great sorrow.

As a Christian, not only can you experience God's peace and comfort when you hurt, but you can also be a channel of that peace and comfort to others who are hurting. It may be through your response to them in their time of suffering, that they experience the love of God that will help to ease their pain and heal their hurt.

Celebrations and Concerns 8 minutes

Ask group members to share any celebrations they have, then any additional concerns for themselves and others.

Closing Prayer 5 minutes

Have group members hold hands during the prayer. Make sure everyone is prayed for by name.

Life Issue

Gossip, swearing, obscene language

Faith Connection

Christians are to be careful about the words they use. Words that intentionally hurt or falsely accuse others, words that demean, words that are obscene, and words that curse God are not consistent with a Christian lifestyle and witness.

Main Ideas

When you know someone who claims to be a Christian and you hear that person gossip about someone else, swear, or use obscene language, that person is sending some confusing signals about his or her faith commitment. Although only God truly knows what's in a person's heart, and you don't want to judge others, you have to wonder about a person's faith maturity and commitment to Christ if that person consistently swears, uses obscenity, or puts down others.

And what about you? If people didn't know you were a Christian, would your choice of words and the way you talk about others make it clear that you follow Jesus Christ? It's difficult in our culture today to not let a few words slip, once in a while. We hear them all the time—from our friends, at school, at home, on the job, in our music, and in the shows and movies we watch. Lyrics and scripts are almost dependent on insults, gossip, and obscenities in order to be marketable. But do we get desensitized to the effects that words can have on us and others?

So what choices do you make as a Christian? This is one of those areas that can be really tough for Christian teenagers, because it will be obvious when you don't join in the gossip, insults, tasteless jokes, and inappropriate language that may seem commonplace around your peers, and maybe even at home.

Here's where you choose to either "talk the talk" (give lip service to your faith) or "walk the walk" (live your faith) through your talk. (Get it?) Ask for God's help and make some intentional decisions about what comes out of your mouth. Be counter-cultural, like Jesus Christ, and use your words to please God and to encourage, heal, and honor others.

Read, Research, Reflect   James 3:5b-10; Ephesians 4:29-31, 5:4, 8-10

Read the Scripture passages and the additional info in your *Synago* Notebook. Make notes on the following:

- Who is speaking or telling the story in each passage? Who is the intended audience? What is the context? (What do you think the situation is? What's happening before and after this passage?)
- Pray about and reflect on the reading. What does it say to you?

Memorize

From the same mouth come blessing and cursing. My brothers and sisters, this ought not to be so.
(James 3:10, NRSV)

Prepare

- Note your own answers to the questions.
- Decide how you'll close in prayer. (See page 28.)
- Get supplies.

Zip the Lip   Session Plan

Opening   **5 minutes**

Welcome/Announcements/Purpose Statement/Prayer

Warm-Up   **5 minutes**

Tell about a time when something you said got you into big trouble. * (For example, your parent caught you cursing and washed your mouth out with soap, or you started a rumor about someone and got nailed for it)

Topic Talk   **20 minutes**

1. Let's talk about gossiping and spreading rumors. Is it a minor or a major problem at your school?

2. (Leader: Remind everyone of the confidential nature of small groups. What's said in the group, stays in the group.)
   a. Without naming names, can you share an incident where gossip or rumors really hurt someone's feelings, ruined his or her reputation, broke up a relationship, or caused some other major fall-out?
   b. Has that ever happened to you, or were you ever guilty of starting a rumor about someone? What happened?

3. How would you define obscenity? Is there a difference between obscene language, vulgar language, or profanity?

4. What do you think about the use of obscenity? Does it annoy you, offend you, turn you off, not bother you, or what? How would you describe your own use of obscenity?

Word Search   James 3:5b-10; Ephesians 4:29-31, 5:4, 8-10   **20 minutes**

Ask a volunteer to read the passage from James.

1. Why do you think the writer of James compares the tongue to a fire?

2. What does it mean to "tame the tongue," and why is it so difficult?

3. According to verses 9–10, why should Christians be concerned with what they say?

Ask another volunteer to read the first passage from Ephesians.

4. How would you rephrase verse 29 in your own words? What are the two types of "talk" mentioned in this verse? Give specific examples of each.

Supplies: *Synago* Notebook for each person, pencils or pens, Bibles or copies of the Bible readings and note cards for those who don't have a *Synago* Notebook

* Questions with an * should be answered by everyone.

5. Verse 30 refers to Christians being "marked" by a "seal"—sort of like carrying a Christian I.D. Christians are marked as people who have been redeemed by God, made new in God's likeness. So, according to the writer, what happens when Christians use obscene and vulgar talk?

Ask a volunteer to read the last passage from Ephesians.

6. What should be a Christian's motivation for choosing what he or she says?

R&R—Reflect and Respond   15 minutes

1. Where is your greatest struggle when it comes to controlling your tongue? (For example, gossip, obscenity) *

2. Does anyone here need to be forgiven for anything that you've said that has hurt God or someone else? We encourage you to share that with the group, if you feel comfortable doing that. (Leader: Confidentiality reminder. Also, if no one responds right away, be patient and give it some time. Be prepared to share your own confession too.)

3. Tell the group one specific thing you will work on regarding your speech, that will make it "more pleasing to the Lord" (Ephesians 5:10).

Wrap-Up   2 minutes

Read aloud, or restate in your own words.

Even for Christians, it is difficult in our culture today to not let a few words slip, once in a while. We hear them all the time—from our friends, at school, at home, on the job, in our music, and in the shows and movies we watch. Lyrics and scripts are almost dependent on insults, gossip, and obscenities in order to be marketable. But do we get desensitized to the effects that words can have on us and others?

So what choices do you make as a Christian? This is one of those areas that can be really tough for Christian teenagers, because it will be obvious when you don't join in the gossip, insults, tasteless jokes, and inappropriate language that may seem commonplace around your peers, and maybe even at home.

Here's where you choose to either "talk the talk" and give lip service to your faith or "walk the walk" and live your faith through the words you choose. So ask for God's help and make some intentional decisions about what comes out of your mouth. Be counter-cultural, like Jesus Christ, and use your words to please God and to encourage, heal, and honor others.

Celebrations and Concerns   5 minutes

Invite group members to share celebrations and concerns.

Closing Prayer   5 minutes

Life Issue

Relating to God

Faith Connection

Jesus Christ taught that the most important thing for Christians to do is to love God. Our love for God should be the essence of who we are and how we live.

Main Ideas

Think of someone you love. What do you feel when you think of that person? How do you show your love to that person? What does it feel like when that person "loves you back"? How painful is it when that person does or says something that hurts you? It's probably not hard for you to answer these questions about a person you love. It becomes more difficult, however, to talk about loving God.

God can seem so "out there" at times, unlike a person you can see, touch, and talk to. Even though you may know in your head and heart that God loves you, you might not know what it's supposed to feel like to love God. And how do you do that? If God is God, why would God even need or want your love? Can you love God without having "loving" feelings?

First of all, it is important to God that we love God. Jesus affirmed the teaching of the Hebrew Scriptures (the Old Testament) that God wants us to love God above all else, with our whole being, and with everything we've got.

The Bible also reveals that God's very nature is love and that God loves each one of us. Understanding how intensely God loves you can be a first step in loving God back. What if you knew that God's love for you was as faithful, passionate, intimate, protective, and devoted as the love that should be between a husband and wife or a parent and child? If we think about God loving us that intensely, we can begin to understand that it means everything to God for us to return God's love.

More than anything, God wants to be in a loving relationship with you, one in which you experience God's love for you and respond by nurturing that relationship and making it the most important one in your life.

Read, Research, Reflect   Matthew 22:34-38; Hosea 2:19-20, 3:1; 1 John 3:1

Read the Scripture passages and the additional info in your *Synago* Notebook. Make notes on the following:

- Who is speaking or telling the story in each passage? Who is the intended audience? What is the context? (What do you think the situation is? What's happening before and after this passage?)
- Pray about and reflect on the reading. What does it say to you?

Memorize

" 'You shall love the Lord your God with all your heart, and with all your soul, and with all your mind.' This is the greatest and first commandment." (Matthew 22:37-38, NRSV)

Prepare

- Note your own answers to the questions.
- Decide how you'll close in prayer. (See page 28.)
- Get supplies.

Loving God   Session Plan

Opening   **5 minutes**

Welcome/Announcements/Purpose Statement/Prayer

Warm-Up   **5 minutes**

Give each person a sheet of paper. Put crayons, colored pencils, or markers within everyone's reach.

When you think of God, what images come to mind? On your sheet of paper, draw your image of God, to the best of your ability. (Stick figures are acceptable.) Write words or phrases around the drawing that describe what you think God is like and what your relationship with God is like.

Topic Talk   **20 minutes**

1. Share your drawing with the group. What is your image of God? What do you think God is like? *

2. Which of the following relationships best describes how you relate to God: *

    a. friend to friend   b. child to parent   c. student to teacher
    d. youth to chaperone   e. accused to judge   f. grandchild to grandparent
    g. servant to master   h. insignificant speck to awesome God
    i. no relationship   j. other (describe)

3. What have been the biggest influences in shaping your image of God and the type of relationship you have with God? *

Word Search   Matthew 22:34-38; Hosea 2:19-20, 3:1; 1 John 3:1   **20 minutes**

Ask a volunteer to read the passage from Matthew.

1. Describe in your own words, what Jesus was asked and how he answered? (If you have different Bible translations or paraphrases, ask volunteers to reread the passage from them.)

2. What do you think it means to love God with
    a. "all your heart"?   b. "all your soul"?   c. "all your mind"?

3. Why do you think Jesus would say that this is the greatest commandment?

Introduce the next two Scripture passages as ones that use metaphors to help us understand what a relationship with God is like. (Remember metaphors? An object, idea, or image that's compared to something else to suggest similarities.) Ask a volunteer to read the passage from Hosea.

4. This Scripture passage uses the metaphor of a marriage (Hosea's) to describe the relationship God has with the Hebrew people. What characteristics of a marriage relationship could we use to describe the loving relationship God wants with us?

Ask a volunteer to read 1 John 3:1.

5. This verse suggests that our relationship with God is like that of a parent and child. If God is a loving parent, what do we know about God's love for us? How could you describe it?

R&R—Reflect and Respond

15 minutes

1. Think about the readings we looked at and discussed. Has anyone gained a new understanding of what God is like, or has anyone's image of God changed? If so, how?

2. What challenges you the most: loving God with all your heart? loving God with all your soul? or loving God with all your mind? And why? *

3. What is one thing you could do to "love God back" or express your love to God?

Wrap-Up

2 minutes

It is important to God that we love God. Jesus affirmed the teaching of the Hebrew Scriptures (the Old Testament) that God wants us to love God above all else, with our whole being, and with everything we've got.

The Bible also reveals that God's very nature is love and that God loves each one of us. Understanding how intensely God loves you can be a first step in loving God back. God's love for you is as faithful, passionate, intimate, protective, and devoted as the love that should be between a husband and wife or a parent and child. If you think about God loving you that intensely, you can begin to understand that it means everything to God for you to return God's love.

More than anything, God wants to be in a loving relationship with you, one in which you experience God's love for you and respond by nurturing that relationship and making it the most important one in your life.

Read aloud, or restate in your own words.

Celebrations and Concerns
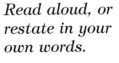
5 minutes

Invite group members to share celebrations and concerns.

Closing Prayer
5 minutes

Life Issue

How I feel about myself and treat myself; self-esteem

Faith Connection

Because God created us and loves us, we should love and care for ourselves. Loving ourselves is reflected in a healthy self-esteem.

Main Ideas

Hey, do you love yourself? Is that a strange question? Doesn't it feel awkward to say, "I love me"? Saying that sounds egotistical. But loving yourself isn't about having a big ego. It's about accepting yourself for who you are—the good and the bad—and caring for yourself—physically, emotionally, mentally, and physically.

Unfortunately, many teenagers question how loveable they really are and experience major drops in self-esteem. "I'm not thin enough." "I'm not cool enough." "I'm not smart enough." "I'm not athletic enough." "I'm not attractive enough." "I'm not good enough." They measure their self-worth against impossible, media standards or the standards of others, and end up loathing themselves, stressing out, or sinking into depression. As they become more self-obsessed, they become less concerned for others, and become even harder on themselves.

Fortunately, God's Word offers hope and encouragement to those of us who find it hard to love ourselves. The Bible tells us that we were created by a loving God for the purpose of being in a loving relationship with the One who created us. Created in love, to be loved. Learn to accept the unconditional, unending, unexplainable, unearnable, unfathomable love of God. When you can accept God's love for you, you are more able to love, appreciate, and care for yourself.

Read, Research, Reflect

Matthew 22:34-39; Psalm 139:13-14

Read the Scripture passages and the additional info in your *Synago* Notebook. Make notes on the following:

- Who is speaking or telling the story in each passage? Who is the intended audience? What is the context? (What do you think the situation is? What's happening before and after this passage?)
- Pray about and reflect on the reading. What does it say to you?

Memorize

" 'You shall love the Lord your God with all your heart, and with all your soul, and with all your mind.' This is the greatest and first commandment." And a second is like it: 'You shall love your neighbor as yourself.' "
(Matthew 22:37-39)

Prepare

- Note your own answers to the questions.
- Decide how you'll close in prayer. (See page 28.)
- Get supplies.

Loving Myself

Opening   5 minutes

Welcome/Announcements/Purpose Statement/Prayer

Warm-Up   5 minutes

Complete the following statement:
"One of the best things I ever did for myself was _____." *

Topic Talk   15 minutes

1. How do you define self-esteem? (Leader tip: Webster's definition of "esteem" is "to have a good opinion of; regard as valuable; respect.")

2. Think about the self-esteem of teenagers at your school. On a scale of one to ten, with ten being very high self-esteem and one being practically nonexistent, where would you rank the self-esteem of the average teenager at your school?

3. Is your own self-esteem higher or lower than what you ranked as the average teen's and why? *

4. What factors do you think significantly affect a teenager's self-esteem?

Word Search   Matthew 22:34-39; Psalm 139:13-14   15 minutes

Ask a volunteer to read the passage from Matthew. Make sure everyone understands the context of the passage and any unfamiliar terms. (If you've already done the session on "Loving God," you'll notice this is the same passage from Matthew, plus verse 39. If you've done "Loving God," just review your earlier responses to questions 1 and 2.)

1. In your own words, what was Jesus being asked and how did he answer?

2. Why do you think Jesus would say that this was the greatest commandment?

Leader: Reread verse 39.

3. What do you think Jesus wanted his listeners to understand when he said to love your neighbor as yourself? Specifically, what do you think he means by loving yourself?

4. Why do you think Jesus ranks this as the second most important commandment? Why does he give it so much priority over other rules for living?

Supplies: *Synago* Notebook for each person, pencils or pens, Bibles or copies of the Bible readings and note cards for those who don't have a *Synago* Notebook

* Questions with an * should be answered by everyone.

Ask a volunteer to read the verses from Psalm 139. If group members have other Bible translations, ask them to read them aloud to the group.

5. What do you think this Scripture reading says about the value of your life? What makes you so valuable?

R&R—Reflect and Respond   25 minutes

1. Do you find it easy, challenging, or impossible to think of yourself as valuable and worthy of love, and why do you think that is?

2. Describe a time or situation when you need to be accepting of yourself , compared to a time or situation when you need to change something about yourself? In other words, what kind of personal changes could you make that come from caring for yourself, rather than from low self-esteem? (Leader: For example, better eating habits and getting exercise could come from caring about yourself; not eating to become and stay thin to match someone else's standards could come from low self-esteem.)

3. Take some time to let group members share words of love, appreciation, and affirmation for one another. Beginning with the person on the leader's left, give two to three group members an opportunity to volunteer to say what they admire and appreciate in that person. Move around the circle until all group members have been affirmed. (Leader: Be prepared to say something positive and affirming about each person, so no one is left out.)

4. Imagine that you are holding yourself as a baby. What words of promise, hope, or encouragement would you say to yourself? What would you promise yourself as a baby, that you will do to care for yourself in the future? * (Leader: Give group members a little time to think about this. Be prepared to go first, as an example.)

Wrap-Up   2 minutes

Read aloud, or restate in your own words.

God's Word offers hope and encouragement to those of us who find it hard to love ourselves. The Bible tells us that we were created by a loving God for the purpose of being in a loving relationship with the One who created us. Created in love, to be loved. Learn to accept the unconditional, unending, unexplainable, unearnable, unfathomable love of God. When you can accept God's love for you, you are more able to love, appreciate, and care for yourself.

Celebrations and Concerns   5 minutes

Invite group members to share celebrations and concerns.

Closing Prayer   5 minutes

Life Issue

Relating to others.

Faith Connection

The Christian faith is one that we live out in our relationships with others. The test of our faith commitment isn't how well we can speak about loving others, but how well we actually love them by meeting their needs. Responding to the needs of others is an expression of our love for God.

Main Ideas

When Jesus and the biblical writers spoke about loving others, they weren't just talking about doing nice things for people every once in a while. They were talking about a radically different way of living and relating to others—a type of lifestyle that ran against the grain of the culture they lived in (and that we live in!). This would be the culture that says, "Don't do something for someone else, unless you get something out of it too."

The first challenge of Christian love is whom we are to love. That's everybody! Not just our buds, sweet old grandmas, favorite teachers, or boyfriends and girlfriends. Anybody can love those people. Christians are called to love, or respond to the needs of, anyone who is in need, regardless of our personal feelings toward that person.

A second challenge is that our love be sacrificial. That means we give of ourselves, in order to respond to the needs of others. Helping someone else may be inconvenient. It may be out of our comfort zone. It may actually cost us in terms of personal energy, money, time, and other resources—even in our image.

Loving others in this way sets us apart as God's people and as followers of Jesus Christ. This lifestyle of loving is not an easy one, nor is it likely to be rewarding in the way our culture defines rewards. Needy people are all around you—every day, everywhere you go. They may be hungry, hurting, or helpless. They may just need someone to listen to them. Or notice them. Maybe you know them. Maybe you don't. Maybe you like them or maybe you can't stand them. It doesn't matter. Just take every opportunity to love others by reaching out to them, as best as you can, and not counting the costs.

Read, Research, Reflect   Luke 10:25-37; 1 John 3:16-18

Read the Scripture passages and the additional info in your *Synago* Notebook. Make notes on the following:

- Who is speaking or telling the story in each passage? Who is the intended audience? What is the context? (What do you think the situation is? What's happening before and after this passage?)
- Pray about and reflect on the reading. What does it say to you?

Memorize

Suppose someone has enough to live and sees a brother or sister in need, but does not help. Then God's love in not living in that person. (1 John 3:17, NCV)

Prepare

- Note your own answers to the questions.
- Decide how you'll close in prayer. (See page 28.)
- Get supplies.

Loving Others

Session Plan

Supplies:
Synago Notebook for each person; pencils or pens; Bibles or copies of the Bible readings and note cards for those who don't have a *Synago* Notebook; a small, soft item, like a stuffed animal, pillow, bean bag, or spongy ball

Opening
5 minutes

Welcome/Announcements/Purpose Statement/Prayer

Warm-Up
3 minutes

Get a small, soft item, like a stuffed animal, pillow, bean bag, or spongy ball. Have group members pass it back and forth across the circle. When the item is caught, the person who caught it must complete the statement: "I love _____." (This could be person, place, thing, whatever.) As soon as that person is finished, he or she throws it to someone else. Keep this going at a pretty fast pace, making sure everyone has had a chance to respond several times. A couple rules: you can't repeat what someone else has said, and you can't throw it back to the person who has just thrown it to you. Use a timer or timekeeper and stop after three minutes.

Topic Talk
15 minutes

* Questions with an * should be answered by everyone.

1. Briefly tell about a time when a total stranger went out of his or her way to help you. How did that experience affect you? *

2. What factors affect whether or not you help someone—time, opportunity, who the person is (or the type of person)? Give examples, if you can.

3. In the movie *Pay It Forward,* a seventh grader decides to try to make the world better by doing random acts of kindness for three people, with the stipulations that they each help three more people and that the acts be challenging or difficult for them to do. Why do you think it mattered that the acts of kindness be personally difficult?

Word Search   Luke 10:25-37; 1 John 3:16-18
25 minutes

(Leader: Give information here about Levites and Samaritans so that group members understand the significance of these characters in the story.)

Ask a volunteer to read the passage from Luke. Note that verses 22-27 parallel Matthew 22:34-37. Read this too.

1. In the passage from Luke, Jesus again answers the "What's the most important commandment?" question, or in this case, how to get eternal life. How was his answer in the Luke passage similar to or different from the passage in Matthew?

2. Briefly describe the characters in the story Jesus told.

3. With this story, what was Jesus trying to teach about who our neighbor is?

4. What was significant about the types of people Jesus used in this story? Why do you think he specifically portrayed two "religious" types as unsympathetic characters and used a cultural outcast as the "good guy"?

5. If the setting for the story were changed to your school campus, who would the characters be? How would you rewrite the story to be relevant to you and your friends?

6. In addition to money what did it "cost" the Samaritan to help the man?

Ask another volunteer to read 1 John 3:16-18.

7. In what ways does this passage summarize the reading from Luke? Anything different?

8. In your own words, what does 1 John 3:16-18 describe as "real love." How is real love practiced?

9. What motivates and enables Christians to really love and help others?

R&R—Reflect and Respond

 15 minutes

1. When it comes to loving others by responding to their needs, what inhibits you the most? What rationale do you use most often for not helping? *

2. Challenge yourself to live a life characterized by random acts of kindness. But, for the next week, focus on one person in your family, church, school, or community to whom you can show kindness. This person's need may be physical, emotional, mental, or spiritual. Helping him or her should involve an investment on your part—of your time, resources, skills, concern, attention. You may not know or like the person. Have you ever heard of the song, "They Will Know We Are Christians by Our Love"? Keep it mind as you decide whom you will focus on helping and how. Share this person's name with the group. *

Wrap-Up

 2 minutes

The first challenge of Christian love is whom we are to love. That's everybody! Not just our buds, sweet old grandmas, favorite teachers, or boyfriends and girlfriends. Anybody can love those people. Christians are called to love, or respond to the needs of, anyone who is in need, regardless of our personal feelings toward that person.

A second challenge is that our love be sacrificial. That means we give of ourselves, in order to respond to the needs of others. Helping someone else may be inconvenient. It may be out of our comfort zone. It may actually cost us in terms of personal energy, money, time, and other resources—even in image.

Loving others in this way sets us apart as God's people and as followers of Jesus Christ. This lifestyle of loving is not an easy one, nor is it likely to be rewarding in the way our culture defines rewards. Needy people are all around you—every day, every where you go. They may be hungry, hurting, or helpless. They may just need someone to listen to them. Or notice them. Maybe you know them. Maybe you don't. Maybe you like them or maybe you can't stand them. It doesn't matter. Just take every opportunity to love others by reaching out to them, as best as you can, and not counting the costs.

Read aloud, or restate in your own words.

Celebrations and Concerns

 5 minutes

Invite group members to share celebrations and concerns.

Closing Prayer

5 minutes

Pray, by name, for those to whom group members will reach out this week.

Loving Others

Life Issue

Feeling hopeless

Faith Connection

Jesus Christ is the light that brings hope and peace to the darkness in our lives and in our world.

Main Ideas

At one time or another, we all live in the dark—not just literal darkness, but the dark that comes and covers us when we feel overwhelmed by pain, despair, sorrow, loneliness, anger—hopelessness. This darkness even extends beyond our own lives, as we consider the hungry, the helpless, and the hurting who fill our world.

Christ was not sent into the world to observe our human misery. He came to experience it and defeat it, so that through faith in him, we can also defeat the darkness that creeps or crashes into our lives. Just as a night light brings a sense of safety, peace, and comfort to a child, so the light of Christ brings hope and peace to our souls. And when his light shines in our own lives, we bring that same hope and peace to a needy and searching world.

Read, Research, Reflect   Isaiah 9:2, 6; John 1:1-9; Psalm 27:1; Matthew 5:14-16

Read the Scripture passages and the additional info in your *Synago* Notebook. Make notes on the following:

- Who is speaking or telling the story in each passage? Who is the intended audience? What is the context? (What do you think the situation is? What's happening before and after this passage?)
- Pray about and reflect on the reading. What does it say to you?

Memorize

You, Lord, are the light that keeps me safe. I am not afraid of anyone. You protect me, and I have no fears.
(Psalm 27:1, CEV)

Prepare

- Note your own answers to the questions.
- Get supplies— don't forget candle(s) and matches for the closing.

Supplies: Candle(s) and matches for closing, *Synago* Notebook for each person, pencils or pens, Bibles or copies of the Bible readings and note cards for those who don't have a *Synago* Notebook

Opening   5 minutes

Welcome/Announcements/Purpose Statement/Prayer

Warm-Up   5 minutes

Were you scared of the dark when you were little? Why? What helped you get over your fears—a night light, stuffed toy, hallway light? *

Topic Talk   15 minutes

1. Darkness can still be a little intimidating, even as you get older. What fears do teenagers and adults associate with darkness?

2. Why does light seem to be a source of comfort when you are in the dark? What positive feelings or experiences do you associate with flashlights, candles, campfires, street lights, and so on?

3. Darkness is also a powerful image we use for conditions in our world. What can darkness refer to, in this sense, and where do you specifically see it in our world today? (Leader tip: poverty, illiteracy, prejudice, injustice, abuse, violence, greed, families breaking apart, apathy, etc. Ask group members to give examples, such as poverty in the Sudan, shootings at schools.)

4. Thinking about yourself, your friends, your family, what types of darkness do individuals experience? * (Leader tip: a lot of the above, plus fear, depression, loneliness, sadness, physical pain, mental illness, addiction)

Word Search   10 minutes

Isaiah 9:2, 6; John 1:1-9; Psalm 27:1; Matthew 5:14-16

Ask volunteers to read aloud the first three Scripture passages.

1. a. Why do you think the writers of these passages used the images of light and darkness? Why would those particular images speak to people?
   b. Is there a different image that might be more meaningful for us today?

2. Many Christians believe that the prophecy in Isaiah foretells the birth of Jesus Christ as the long-awaited Messiah of the Hebrew people, and that John the Baptist, mentioned in the second reading, also announced the coming of Jesus as the Messiah. The term "Lord" in Psalm 27:1 could also be interpreted as a reference to God or Jesus.

   With all that in mind, read these three passages silently, for what they can tell us about the nature of Jesus Christ. Think of a word or phrase to describe Jesus—one that stuck with you from the readings or one you come up with on your own. (Leader tip: *light, child, son, hope, had authority, counselor, God, eternal, like a Father, rules in peace, was with God, all things created through him, safe, protector*) Tell the group your word. *

* Questions with an * should be answered by everyone.

Light in the Dark

Ask a volunteer to read aloud Matthew 5:14-16.

3. Jesus, who refers to himself in Scripture as the Light (John 8:12), tells his followers that they are also light. What do you think he means by this? What is the light of Christ?

R&R—Reflect and Respond

10 minutes

1. Thinking about the darkness that exists in our world, what is a way that you can shine the light of Christ? Or do you feel the darkness, or the problem, is too big or difficult?

2. Who are some individuals who have brought the light of Christ—Christ's love, peace, and hope—into your life in some way? *

3. Do you know someone who is experiencing his or her own darkness, for whom you can bring the light of Christ? How can you try to do that?

Sharing Out of Our Darkness

20 minutes

Light a candle in the center of the group—other candles may also be lit in the room—and turn off the lights. If you are leading this session during the church season of Advent, you can say that Advent is the season of the Christian year when we prepare to celebrate the birth of Christ, remembering him as the Light who came into our world. Read aloud the following:

Read aloud, or restate in your own words.

At one time or another, we all live in the dark—not just literal darkness, but the dark that comes and covers us when we feel overwhelmed by pain, despair, sorrow, loneliness, anger—hopelessness. This darkness even extends beyond our own lives, as we consider the hungry, the helpless, and the hurting who fill our world.

Christ was not sent into the world to observe our human misery. He came to experience it and defeat it, so that through faith in him, we can also defeat the darkness that creeps or crashes into our lives. Just as a night light brings a sense of safety, peace, and comfort to a child, so the light of Christ brings hope and peace to our souls. And when his light shines in our own lives, we bring that same hope and peace to a needy and searching world.

This candle reminds us that Jesus Christ entered our world to bring hope and healing and is present with us now. We know that each of us is either going through a time of darkness in our lives or we are close to someone who is. In this safe and loving circle, may we have a time of safe and honest sharing, where we expose whatever darkness we are experiencing to the loving light of Christ in this group.

Encourage group members to share any sadness or pain or hopelessness in their lives or in the lives of people they care about. Be patient with silence. (Leader tip: Be prepared to start.)

Closing Prayer

10 minutes

Invite group members to hold hands and pray silently as you read aloud the first three Bible passages. Then invite them to pray aloud for those who have spoken of their need. Leader closes, to make sure all who have shared have been prayed for by name. End the prayer with words of thanks and praise to God for Jesus Christ, the comforting hope and light of our world.